James Ramsden is a 29-year-old food writer, cook, and knife-for-hire. He has written about food and cookery for the *Guardian, The Times*, the *FT, delicious., Sainsbury's Magazine, London Evening Standard* and many others. His supper club, the Secret Larder, is one of the most popular in London and was described by one journalist as 'harder to get into than the Ivy.' He has built a reputation for creating exciting, trendy, tasty food *without* the gaga gourmet, and yet he is also known for his relaxed and sociable presence amongst the guests. He is the author of *Small Adventures in Cooking* and two other Pavilion titles, *Do-ahead Dinners* (2012) and *Love Your Lunchbox* (2014).

Praise for *Do-ahead Dinners*:

'This is a book you really want. No fifteen minute magic or culinary sorcery, just practical, staged cooking of the most sumptuous dishes. The style is as lighthearted and enticing as the food. All you need for stress-less kitchen loitering.' *Yotam Ottolenghi*

'James Ramsden's writing is so compelling and his recipes so accessible that *Do-ahead Dinners* made me want to run straight into the kitchen and start cooking. His is a refreshing, distinctive and authoritative voice in contemporary food writing.' *Russell Norman of Polpo*

'It's fantastic. I want to cook every single thing in it.' *India Knight*

DO-AHEAD
CHRISTMAS

DO-AHEAD
CHRISTMAS

James Ramsden

photography by Clare Winfield

PAVILION

FOR MUM, WHO MAKES CHRISTMAS PERFECT,
AND MY FAMILY, WHO DESPITE THEIR BEST EFFORTS DO TOO.

CONTENTS

INTRODUCTION

For many of us Christmas is defined, above all, by food. Carols and stockings and Messiahs in mangers all have their place, but when it comes down to it, the festive period is measured in meals. It tastes of citrus fruit and spice, smoked salmon and roast ham, sweet sherry and sprouts. Food and drink slink their way into almost every aspect of Christmas ritual – the tangerine at the bottom of the stocking, the dolly mix-studded orange at Christingle, slurps of mulled wine while merrily ding-donging on high, and of course the meals themselves. Food is the backbone of Christmas.

It is no surprise, then, that with this gastronomic emphasis comes a certain amount of stress, worry and pressure. More often than not there are many mouths to feed and bellies to please. And because this is a special time of year, we, as cooks, feel the food needs to live up to expectations – or, better still, to surpass them. Yet there's also the quiet compulsion to keep with tradition – for the mince pies to taste as good as they used to, for there to be turkey even if half the people assembled don't like it, and for whatever other festive quirks each family has to remain firmly in place.

In short, it's a minefield. Furthermore, it's a minefield that is littered with manifold other distractions – people dropping in, presents to wrap, children to entertain, an endless procession of things that need doing. You don't, ideally, want to find yourself elbow-deep in currants, kitchen bathed in dripping, and oven stacked with mince pies. You want to have it all done already. Which is where this book comes in.

Each recipe is written with the purpose of giving you as few last-minute kitchen jobs as possible. Some recipes can be done well ahead and stored in a cupboard; some months ahead and frozen. Most give you a day or two's breathing space. All, I hope, taste like Christmas.

There is not a small amount of trepidation in writing a Christmas cookery book. Even those with the most indifferent eating habits the rest of the year will have some fairly robust and unshakeable views on how such-and-such a dish should be. I've tried to balance tradition with a touch of innovation – enough novelty to keep things interesting, enough convention not to rock the boat.

Above all, I want this book to guide your own Christmas. You don't *have* to follow these recipes. By all means do Christmas just as you always have (for some that's what Christmas is about). But I hope the methods I suggest and the general spirit of this book will help make your Christmas cooking easier. As far as I'm concerned, the more time you've got for family, friends and fizz, the better.

HOW TO USE THE RECIPES

A book that incorporated all of the Christmas recipes from across the globe would be more akin to an encyclopedia than a cookery book. This is predominantly a British Christmas cookery book, with a whisper of the American inherited from my mother, and a dash of the Scandinavian from my grandmother. And my wife. Who isn't Scandinavian, but wishes she were.

Each recipe is broken down into stages based on how far ahead it can be done, with a maximum time and a minimum time, followed by the instructions for finishing the dish. Naturally this isn't exhaustive, and at this time of year in particular it's often handy to snatch 5 minutes here and there to sweat some onions, or make some pastry. As ever, the best method is to read the recipe in full before starting so that you can work out the most practical way forward for you. And make sure you've got all the kit.

Few of these dishes involve fiddly prep or rarified techniques. But some might require the radio and a cup of tea to help them along. If you enjoy cooking then that shouldn't be a great hardship. If you only just put up with cooking then maybe that cup of tea should be something a little stronger.

COOKING FOR NUMBERS

While a deluge of guests, announced or otherwise, is part of the deal at this time of year, it seemed impractical to tailor every recipe to the eventuality of having 20 mouths to feed. Most of these recipes serve 6–8 people, with the odd exception of a terrine, turkey, or trifle. Cooks tend to get their knickers in a twist about scaling recipes up, or indeed down, but for the most part it's straightforward.

As a general rule of thumb, divide ingredients by the number of servings, then multiply up: i.e. if a recipe that serves 6 asks for 750g beef, that's 125g per person, so if you're feeding 10 people, then you need 1.25kg beef. That said, certain ingredients don't demand this – base ingredients like onions, garlic, spices and herbs can make themselves known without being scaled up or down. If halving a recipe you don't need to start halving cinnamon sticks.

Wherever scaling isn't straightforward I've made a note of that, though when in doubt, you're best off cooking in separate batches.

Keep in mind that in greater quantities things may take more time to prep and to cook, that you'll need bigger pots and pans, and that reheating may also take longer.

ON FREEZING

Not only can many of these recipes be done several days ahead, but a good number can also be frozen. If freezing, make sure you leave to cool completely first, then wrap thoroughly and freeze. Unless the recipe specifies reheat from frozen, defrost overnight in the fridge, or in a cool, dry place, and reheat as in the recipe.

IF YOU NEED ANY HELP

Should you have any questions or concerns, please do get in touch. You can reach me on email at james@jamesramsden.com, or via Twitter @jteramsden, or using the hashtag #DoAheadChristmas.

Cook your Christmas stockings off.

A FEW MENU SUGGESTIONS

A DRINKS PARTY

Mulled wine (p.14)
Prosecco with elderflower, orange and rosemary (p.24)
Tangerine whiskey sour (p.20)

Chorizo, olives and pickled chilli (p.30)
Christmas koftas (p.33)
Hasselback potatoes with sour cream and caviar (p.44)
Roasted pepper and almond dip (p.41)

FESTIVE DINNER FOR THE RUN-UP TO CHRISTMAS

Hot brown buttered rum (p.16)

Salmon ceviche toasts (p.36)

Chilli nuts (p.34)

Herb-stuffed leg of lamb with watercress and anchovy sauce (p.66)
Coffee-roasted beetroot with horseradish and buttermilk dressing
and toasted hazelnuts (p.59)

Apple snow with fennel biscuits (p.74)

CHRISTMAS DAY
(see p.80)

BOXING DAY LUNCH

*To be done, ideally, well in advance so that
you can operate on autopilot on the day.*

Sloegasm (p.24)

Roast garlic, Parmesan and anchovy pastries (p.38)

Pickled herring and spiced onion on rye (p.54)

Guinness and marmalade ham with celeriac dauphinois (p.62)

Chocolate, orange and hazelnut tart (p.76)

NEW YEAR'S EVE

*On NYE there is nowhere better to be than in your own home,
eating good food, drinking passable wine, and within flopping
distance of your own bed.*

Prosecco with elderflower, orange and rosemary (p.24)

Polenta chips with blue cheese sauce (p.35)
Prawn and mango salad (p.46)
Smoked aubergine and walnut dip (p.40)

Fish soup (p.56)

Venison wellington with roast onions and Époisses cheese (p.60)

Tangerine granita (p.73)

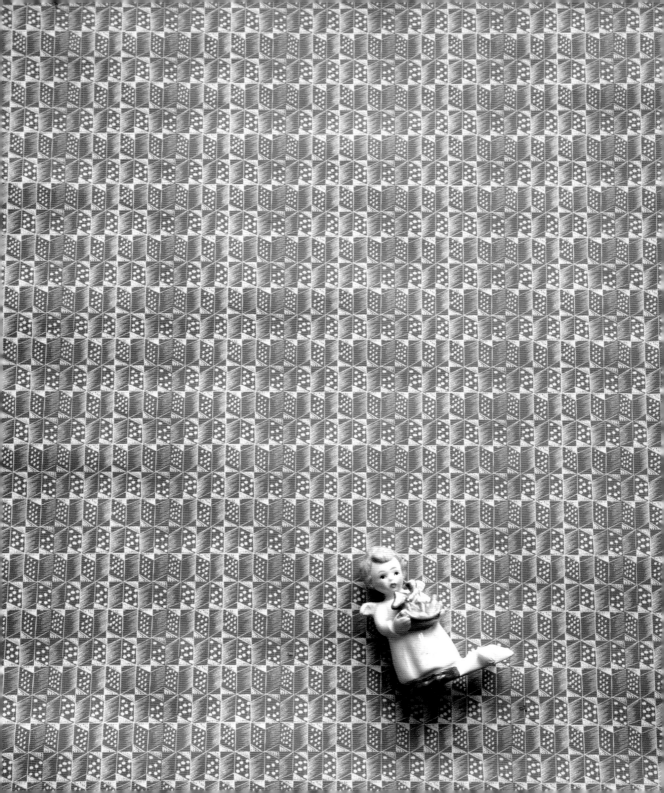

DRINKS

There is a whole boozy realm of festive cocktails beyond the old favourites of mulled wine and cheap fizz. And while here I barely scratch the surface of the global Christmas drinks binge – that could be a whole other book – I'm hoping these at least bring with them the cut and thrust of Advent hooch. In a fit of over-exuberance (and, of course, in the interests of rigorous testing) I served them all at a party last Christmas. My memory of the evening is, consequently, a little hazy, though I think it wouldn't be inaccurate to say that they all went down famously. There was certainly a moment while I was dancing on the kitchen table when I thought: 'those tangerine whiskey sours are *brilliant*.'

It's not all hard liquor, mind – lambswool is a very mellow, medieval mulled ale and apple drink, and there are even a couple of non-alcoholic cocktails for the drivers.

Chin chin.

MULLED WINE

MAKES 24 SERVINGS
zest and juice of
   1 large orange
300g/10½oz/1½ cups caster
   (superfine) sugar
a few strips of lemon peel
2 cinnamon sticks
4 star anise
5 cardamom pods, squashed
   with the flat of a knife
5 cloves
5 slices of fresh ginger
a little grated nutmeg
300ml/10fl oz/1¼ cups water
4 bottles of young, fruity
   red wine
a large glass of brandy
   (optional)

Mulled wine is the definitive Christmas cocktail. When it's good it really is rather lovely, and when it's bad, well, it keeps you warm and is unnoticeable after a couple. Nevertheless, I think this recipe falls into the first category – not too sweet, lightly spiced, a whiff of citrus … Christmas in a glass (or mug). Worth making a big batch.

UP TO 1 WEEK AHEAD (MIN. 1 HOUR)
Put the orange juice and zest, sugar, lemon peel and spices in a large saucepan with the water and bring to a boil, stirring to dissolve the sugar. Simmer gently for 5 minutes and then leave to infuse for up to a week.

UP TO 1 HOUR AHEAD (MIN. 30 MINUTES)
Mix the wine and spiced syrup – with the brandy if using – in a large saucepan and warm over a low heat. Don't boil, but quietly bring it up to hot-cup-of-tea temperature and let it tick over for at least 20 minutes. Serve in heatproof glasses or mugs, or decant into a thermos flask.

CHEAT: If doing at the last minute, don't bother with the spice syrup – bung it all in a pan and stir as you heat it up to dissolve the sugar.

SCALING UP: You don't need to go OTT on the spices. Add sugar to taste.

HOT BROWN BUTTERED RUM

SERVES 6

50g/1¾oz/4 tbsp unsalted
    butter
3 tbsp soft brown sugar
1 tsp mixed spice
200ml/7fl oz/generous ¾ cup
    golden rum
300ml/10fl oz/1¼ cups dry
    cider
6 cinnamon sticks

Hot buttered rum must be one of the most inviting-sounding drinks on the planet. It evokes images of fireplaces and blankets and makes my chest swell just thinking of it. I've added the smallest of twists here by browning the butter first, which imparts a pleasant nutty richness to the affair.

UP TO 1 WEEK AHEAD (MIN. 10 MINUTES):
Melt the butter in a saucepan over a medium heat and cook, stirring occasionally, until nut brown. Hold your nerve – the further you take the butter the better – but take care not to burn. Add the sugar and spice, stirring to combine, and cook for 2 minutes. Set aside and cool until needed.

UP TO 30 MINUTES AHEAD:
Remelt the spiced butter if necessary and add the rum, cider and cinnamon. Warm over a gentle heat until approaching a boil. Whisk thoroughly, then strain into glasses or mugs. Serve garnished with a cinnamon stick.

SCALING UP: Only add ½ tsp mixed spice for each time you double the quantities.

BOURBON AND MAPLE EGGNOG

SERVES 6

300ml/10fl oz/1¼ cups
    bourbon
3 tbsp maple syrup
3 tbsp double (heavy) cream
4 eggs
200ml/7fl oz/generous ¾ cup
    whole milk
ice
nutmeg

This is one of those quintessential American holiday drinks that you hear people talk about but never *quite* know what it is. Or at least that was the case for me. The idea of egg in a cocktail ain't that appealing, either. And yet this is a quite sumptuous beverage, a boozy custard that slips down quicker than a spaniel on ice.

If you want to serve this warm, omit the ice and warm through gently in a microwave or on the hob.

UP TO 2 HOURS AHEAD:
Put the bourbon, maple syrup, cream, eggs and milk in a cocktail shaker and shake vigorously. Chill.

30 MINUTES AHEAD:
Put 6 glasses in the freezer.

TO SERVE:
Give the eggnog another shake with a few ice cubes, then strain into glasses and finish with a little grating of nutmeg.

CHESTNUT BRANDY PUNCH

SERVES 6
50g/1¾oz cooked chestnuts,
    roughly chopped
100ml/3½fl oz/7 tbsp double
    (heavy) cream
300ml/10fl oz/1¼ cups brandy
150ml/5fl oz/⅔ cup crème de
    cacao or other chocolate
    liqueur
ice
nutmeg

This is a brandy Alexander, essentially, given a Christmas twist with the addition of chestnuts that may or may not be roasted on an open fire. In fact, they aren't, or at least not when I make this recipe – I use those perfectly decent vacuum-packed chestnuts.

UP TO 1 WEEK AHEAD (MIN. 1 HOUR):
Gently warm the chestnuts in a pan with the cream until just below simmering point. Tip into a blender and blend until smooth, pass through a sieve into a small bowl, then leave to cool. Chill in the fridge, or freezer if in a hurry.

30 MINUTES AHEAD:
Put 6 cocktail glasses or small tumblers in the freezer.

TO SERVE:
Shake together the chestnut cream, brandy and crème de cacao with a few ice cubes. Strain into the chilled glasses, and finish with a grating of nutmeg.

TANGERINE WHISKEY SOUR

SERVES 6

zest of 2 tangerines
100ml/3½fl oz/7 tbsp
    tangerine juice
100ml/3½fl oz/7 tbsp lemon
    juice
50g/1¾oz/¼ cup caster
    (superfine) sugar
300ml/10fl oz/1¼ cups
    bourbon
1 egg white
6 strips of orange peel
dash of Angostura or
    orange bitters

The whiskey sour is a fine cocktail – deliciously tart, yet rich, with those wonderful vanilla, caramel notes found in a good bourbon. A Christmas twist comes with the addition of orange peel and tangerine juice.

UP TO 1 DAY AHEAD (MIN. 2 HOURS):

Put the tangerine zest and juice, lemon juice and sugar in a small pan and bring to a boil, stirring to dissolve the sugar. Simmer for 3 minutes, then strain into a jug and chill.

30 MINUTES AHEAD:

Put 6 tumblers in the freezer.

TO SERVE:

Fill your chilled tumblers with ice. Thoroughly whisk the tangerine syrup together with the bourbon and egg white. Strain into the glasses. Garnish with orange peel, add a dash of bitters, and serve.

SCALING UP: With a good shake or whisk, a little egg white goes a long way, so no need to go OTT with that.

LAMBSWOOL

SERVES 6

200g/7oz/1 cup caster (superfine) sugar
200ml/7fl oz/generous ¾ cup water
1 tbsp grated fresh ginger
2 cloves
2 cardamom pods, lightly crushed
2 cooking apples, peeled, cored and roughly chopped
100g/3½oz/½ cup soft brown sugar
2 tsp ground cinnamon
a good grating of nutmeg
750ml/1¼ pints/3 cups IPA or light ale
150ml/5fl oz/⅔ cup Calvados or brandy (optional)

I first encountered this hearty medieval drink when I asked the readers of my blog to suggest some quirky Christmas dishes. This is indeed quirky, a sort of mulled beer that was quaffed by the flagon way back when. It is both delicious and relatively low in alcohol, and therefore handy for those who are driving. For those who aren't, a slug of Calvados or brandy will give it more of a kick.

UP TO 1 WEEK AHEAD (MIN. 1 HOUR):

Put the caster sugar, water, ginger, cloves and cardamom in a small pan and bring to a boil, stirring to dissolve the sugar. Simmer for 3 minutes and set aside.

Put the apples, brown sugar, cinnamon and nutmeg in a pan with a splash of water. Cover and cook over a medium heat for 10–15 minutes, until the apples have collapsed. Blend until smooth. Strain the spice syrup into the apples and set aside.

UP TO 1 HOUR AHEAD (MIN. 30 MINUTES):

Put the beer and the spiced apple syrup in a pan and warm over a gentle heat. Don't boil. Serve in warmed glasses or mugs, with a splash of Calvados if you like.

SCALING UP: Go easy on the cinnamon, using about 1 tsp for each time you double the recipe.

PROSECCO WITH ELDERFLOWER, ORANGE AND ROSEMARY

SERVES 6

6 tsp elderflower cordial
6 sprigs of rosemary
6 slivers of orange peel
a bottle of Prosecco, chilled

An incredibly straightforward but elegant way of pepping up your Christmas fizz. You could use Cava or indeed Champagne for this, though I do think Prosecco's floral notes of lemon and apple make it the most appropriate bevvy.

AHEAD, IF YOU LIKE:
Put a teaspoon of elderflower cordial in the bottom of each glass, along with a sprig of rosemary and a sliver of orange peel.

TO SERVE:
Fill each glass with Prosecco, give a little stir, and serve.

SLOEGASM

SERVES 6

6–12 tbsp sloe gin (according to taste)
a bottle of Champagne or Cava, chilled

Forgive the bawdy name of this cocktail but it's the only one I've known it to be given. Actually, *Difford's Guide*, the only cocktail book you'll ever need, calls it Sloe Motion – but I couldn't steal their moniker. So here we are. A perfect union of sloe gin and Champagne. English sparkling wine tallies up well, but even Cava will do the trick. Prosecco may be too sweet but it's going to be pretty drinkable whatever you use. Fire some Blue Nun into the SodaStream and see if anyone notices.

AHEAD, IF YOU LIKE:
Put a tablespoon or two of sloe gin in the bottom of your Champagne flutes.

TO SERVE:
Top up with Champagne and serve.

PEAR AND STAR ANISE VIRGIN FIZZ

SERVES 6

500ml/18fl oz/generous 2 cups
   pear (or pear and apple)
   juice
juice of 1 lemon
6 star anise
1 cinnamon stick
6 slices of lemon
ice
soda water

It's a rum time of year for those who, for whatever reason, are off the grog. Cocktails and fizz spraying this way and that and nary a glass of water for the teetotaller. So it's nice to make something delicious and festive for them. Add gin for a kick.

UP TO 1 DAY AHEAD (MIN. 2 HOURS):

Gently warm the pear juice, lemon juice, star anise and cinnamon in a saucepan until just under a boil. Take off the heat and leave to infuse for at least 1 hour. Chill.

TO SERVE:

Put a star anise and a slice of lemon in each glass along with a handful of ice. Half-fill with the pear juice and top up with fizzy water.

APPLE, GINGER AND CRANBERRY VIRGIN COCKTAIL

SERVES 6

ice
1 litre/1¾ pints/4 cups apple
   juice
1 litre/1¾ pints/4 cups
   cranberry juice
3 tbsp ginger cordial
6 sprigs of mint
6 slices of lemon

Ginger and apple make terrific bedfellows. Cranberry is the icing on the cake. I left a jug of this out at a Christmas party and guests were merrily slurping away at it for some time before being informed that it didn't actually have alcohol in it. Like they subsequently did, you can add vodka.

Fill a large jug with ice and add the apple juice, cranberry juice and ginger cordial. Give it a good stir, then pour into glasses. Garnish with a sprig of mint and a slice of lemon.

PARTY BITES

I have yet to come up with an appealing name for the things you eat with drinks: 'canapés' sounds too formal, 'nibbles' too twee, 'snacks' too grabby, 'eats' too … vague. I've landed on 'party bites' because at least it conveys what these are. If you come up with a better name, answers on a postcard.

Moving on … Good things to eat with drinks are arguably what turn a nice party into a memorable one. They're a conversation starter, an appetite-whetter, and a general pepper-upper of any frolic. This is by no means to suggest that they ought or need to be complicated, but a touch of effort beyond crisps and dip (noble as they are) is almost always worth it.

The problem usually comes in the frantic assembly of these things while everyone is starting to arrive. It's not what a host needs. The following recipes can all be prepared ahead, and most completed ahead, with a few just needing a bit of reheating here, a dollop of something there – the sort of thing that a friend or child isn't going to hash up too badly.

In terms of servings, the general rule of thumb is that people eat 6–7 bits if they're off out for dinner afterwards, more like 10–12 if not, and 15–20 if their surname is Ramsden. That said, I almost always find I've made too much, as opposed to too little, so as a rule of thumb it's perhaps a little vague. Either that or I don't have as many friends as I thought. Could be that.

Last thing: seasoning. Because you only get one, at most two, mouthfuls of each thing, you want to err on the side of over-seasoning. These morsels need to sing.

CHORIZO, OLIVES AND PICKLED CHILLI

MAKES ABOUT 30
1 tsp olive oil

500g/1lb 2oz piece of sweet (dulce) chorizo, cut into fat chunks

100ml/3½fl oz/7 tbsp fino sherry

150–200g/5½–7oz small pitted green olives

pickled guindilla peppers (Spanish green chilli peppers), available in large supermarkets), cut into small pieces

a handful of parsley, roughly chopped

This is incredibly simple but I know few people who don't go weak at the knees for a bit of hot chorizo. Hot olives are a newish one on me, but a newish favourite at that. They're considerably more bewitching when warm.

UP TO 1 DAY AHEAD (MIN. 30 MINUTES):

Heat the oil in an ovenproof frying pan and fry the chorizo on both sides until crisp – about 2 minutes each side. Add the sherry and simmer for a few minutes, until reduced by about half. Take off the heat and leave to cool slightly.

Put a cocktail stick through an olive, then through a slice of pickled chilli, and then through a piece of chorizo, and stand upright in the frying pan. When you have speared all the chorizo, cover the pan and store somewhere cool.

30 MINUTES AHEAD:

Preheat the oven to 200°C/400°F/Gas mark 6. Put the pan in the oven for 5–7 minutes to warm the chorizo and olives. Scatter with parsley and serve.

SCALING UP: If you only have a small frying pan you'll need to do this in batches. Reheat on a baking tray.

CHRISTMAS KOFTAS

500g/1lb 2oz minced (ground) lamb
250g/9oz minced (ground) pork
1 onion, very finely chopped
3 tbsp pine nuts, toasted and finely chopped
1 tbsp ras-el-hanout
1 tsp ground cinnamon
a good handful of parsley, finely chopped
1 egg, beaten
salt and pepper
olive oil
150ml/5½fl oz/⅔ cup sour cream
a handful of pomegranate seeds
coriander (cilantro) leaves

I tend to avoid fiddly nibbles or food-in-miniature, but if there were ever a time of year for a bit of kitsch, it's Christmas. There is no way these little fellas won't raise a smile.

UP TO 2 DAYS AHEAD (MIN. 1 HOUR):
Mix the lamb, pork, onion, pine nuts, spices, parsley and egg and season generously with salt and pepper. Fry a little piece of the mixture and taste for seasoning, adding a little more salt if necessary. Form into 30 or so walnut-sized balls and chill for 30 minutes.

Preheat the oven to 200°C/400°F/Gas mark 6. Heat a little oil in a large non-stick frying pan and fry the balls in batches for 5 minutes, turning occasionally, until nicely browned, then transfer to a baking tray. Bake in the oven for 5–7 minutes, until firm and cooked, then set aside to cool. Cover and chill or freeze until needed.

30 MINUTES AHEAD:
Preheat the oven to 200°C/400°F/Gas mark 6. Bake the koftas for 10 minutes, or 15 minutes from frozen. Rest for a few minutes, then garnish with a blob of sour cream, a pomegranate seed and a coriander leaf before serving.

FREEZABLE
CHEAT: Buy ready-made spicy meatballs and garnish as above.
SCALING UP: Go easy on the onion and egg if doubling quantities.

CHILLI NUTS

MAKES A LARGE JAR'S WORTH

250g/9oz/2 cups mixed
    nuts – pecans, cashews,
    blanched almonds
50g/1¾oz/4 tbsp unsalted
    butter
25g/1oz/2 tbsp caster
    (superfine) sugar
½ tsp chilli powder
zest of 1 lime
sea salt flakes

Who can resist a nut? Nut allergy sufferers obviously, but other than that? They're salty and crunchy and perfect with a drink. A jar of these would make a lovely present too.

UP TO 1 WEEK AHEAD (MIN. 1 HOUR):

Put a large frying pan over a high heat and add the nuts. Cook, shuggling the pan regularly, until toasted and fragrant – about 5 minutes. Take care not to burn. Tip the nuts into a bowl and add the butter to the pan. Once melted add the sugar, chilli powder and lime zest and stir until the sugar has dissolved. Return the nuts to the pan along with a pinch of salt and cook for another 3–4 minutes, stirring almost constantly, until well-coated and glistening. Tip onto kitchen paper and leave until cool. Add a good pinch of sea salt and store in a sterilized jar (see note on p.200) until needed.

SCALING UP: Go easy on the chilli powder.

POLENTA CHIPS WITH BLUE CHEESE SAUCE

SERVES 20
1 litre/1¾ pints/4 cups water
salt and pepper
250g/9oz/2 cups quick-cook
    polenta (cornmeal)
4 tbsp olive oil
For the blue cheese sauce
20g/¾oz/1½ tbsp butter
1 garlic clove, crushed to
    a paste
200g/7oz Gorgonzola,
    crumbled
100ml/3½fl oz/7 tbsp sour
    cream

A dish inspired by Gail's Kitchen in London. They could have served me utter garbage for the rest of the meal and I would have gone back for these. Thankfully they didn't.

UP TO 3 DAYS AHEAD (MIN. 3 HOURS):
In a large pan, bring the water to a boil, add a pinch of salt and then slowly add the polenta, whisking all the while to prevent lumps forming. Cook according to packet instructions, stirring regularly. Tip onto a baking sheet lined with clingfilm and flatten. Cool, then cover and chill in the fridge until completely set.

Preheat the oven to 200°C/400°F/Gas mark 6. Brush a baking sheet – or two – with a little of the oil. Turn the polenta onto a board and slice into pieces about the size of a domino. Place on the baking sheet, then rub with the remaining oil. Season with salt and pepper. Bake in the oven for 55–60 minutes until crisp and golden. Cool and chill or freeze.

To make the sauce, melt the butter in a pan and add the garlic. Cook over a low heat until soft, then add the Gorgonzola and sour cream, and cook, stirring regularly, until the cheese has melted. Season with pepper, cover and chill or freeze.

30 MINUTES AHEAD:
Preheat the oven to 200°C/400°F/Gas mark 6.

15 MINUTES AHEAD:
Put the polenta chips in the oven for 5–7 minutes to warm up, or 12–15 minutes from frozen. Very gently warm the sauce in a pan or in the microwave (if this is done too hastily the sauce will split).

TO SERVE:
Dribble the sauce over the chips and serve.

FREEZABLE
SCALING: The ratio for polenta is always one part polenta to four parts water – scale up and down at will.

SALMON CEVICHE TOASTS

MAKES ABOUT 30

1 ciabatta loaf

500g/1lb 2oz fresh salmon, skinned

3 tbsp very finely chopped shallot

2 red chillies, deseeded and very finely chopped

juice of 2 limes

1 tsp sesame oil

2 tsp light soy sauce

coriander (cilantro) leaves or microherbs to garnish

There are all manner of means of mucking about with smoked salmon, though in all honesty I'm not convinced you can do much better than the classic brown bread-butter-lemon combo. So this uses unsmoked salmon, and mucks around with it to great effect, if I say so myself.

You can find microherbs such as coriander, cress and amaranth more easily these days, which make a very pretty garnish. Fresh coriander works well otherwise.

UP TO 6 HOURS AHEAD (MIN. 2 HOURS):

Preheat the oven to 200°C/400°F/Gas mark 6. Slice the ciabatta as thinly as you can (it helps if you freeze it for an hour first). Lay on a baking sheet and bake for 5 minutes, until toasted. Place on a wire rack and leave to cool and crisp.

Dice the salmon into 1cm/½in cubes, then cover and chill. Mix the shallot, chillies, lime juice, sesame oil and soy sauce and set aside.

30 MINUTES AHEAD:

Combine the salmon with the shallot and chilli marinade. Taste for seasoning and add a pinch of salt if necessary. Cover and set aside.

10 MINUTES AHEAD:

Spoon the salmon onto the toasts. Garnish with coriander or microherbs. Serve.

ROAST GARLIC, PARMESAN AND ANCHOVY PASTRIES

MAKES 24
a bulb of garlic
salt and pepper
olive oil
50g/1¾oz Parmesan, grated
100g/3½oz jar of anchovies,
    drained
4 tbsp olive oil
500g/1lb 2oz puff pastry
1 egg, beaten

These moreish, if vampire-scattering, pastries are somewhat retro, but in no way worse off for it. Roasting the garlic takes the edge off, so don't be tempted to skip this step, though perhaps do plan ahead enough to do this when the oven's on for another purpose – it seems a bit wasteful to fire up the oven just to roast some garlic.

UP TO 1 WEEK AHEAD (MIN. 2 HOURS):
Preheat the oven to 200°C/400°F/Gas mark 6. Slice the top quarter off the bulb of garlic to expose the cloves within. Season with salt and pepper, add a splosh of oil, and wrap up in a sheet of foil. Roast for 45–50 minutes, until soft and golden.

Cool for a few minutes, then squish out the cloves, discarding the papery skin. Mash or blend the garlic with the Parmesan and anchovies, seasoning with a twist more pepper. Cover and store in the fridge until needed.

UP TO 2 DAYS AHEAD (MIN. 1 HOUR)
Roll out the pastry into a rectangle 2mm/⅟₁₆in thick. Spread with the garlic and anchovy paste. Roll the pastry up like a sleeping bag and slice into roughly 1cm/½in thick rounds. Lay on a lightly floured baking sheet, cover and chill. Meanwhile, preheat the oven to 180°C/350°F/Gas mark 4. Brush the pastries with beaten egg and bake for 20 minutes, until puffed and golden. Serve, or cover and chill, or freeze until needed.

TO REHEAT:
Preheat the oven to 200°C/400°F/Gas mark 6 and reheat for 7 minutes from chilled, or 12 minutes from frozen. Serve.

FREEZABLE

HOT BUTTERED CRAB TOASTS

MAKES 20

100g/3½oz/7 tbsp unsalted
　　butter
1 garlic clove, crushed to
　　a paste
300g/10½oz white crab meat
200g/7oz brown crab meat
juice of 1 lemon
a small grating of nutmeg
a few good shakes
　　of Tabasco
salt and pepper
5 or so slices of good-quality
　　bread

This is in every way a treat: rich, decadent, not exactly kind on
the wallet, worth every penny.

UP TO 1 DAY AHEAD (MIN. 30 MINUTES):

Melt the butter in a saucepan over a low heat, add the garlic
and gently cook for a minute or two until the kitchen smells all
garlicky, then add the crab, lemon juice, nutmeg and Tabasco.
Season with salt and pepper and cook for another few minutes,
stirring regularly. Taste for seasoning, then leave to cool. Store in
the fridge until needed.

UP TO 3 HOURS AHEAD (MIN. 30 MINUTES):

Lightly toast the bread.

20 MINUTES AHEAD:

Preheat the grill to high. Slather the buttered crab over the toast
and put under the grill for 2–3 minutes, until starting to colour. Cut
into attackable pieces and serve.

THREE DIPS FOR CRISPS, CROUTONS AND CRUDITÉS

There are times for fiddling about with pretty canapés, and there are times when you just need something for the masses to descend upon with tortilla chips, or pieces of toast, or bits of vegetable. These dippy, spready numbers are for those moments.

If you fancy making your own crisp things, then buy a load of pitta breads, hack them into little triangles, toss in olive oil, salt and smoked paprika, and bake in the oven at 200°C/400°F/Gas mark 6 until crisp and golden.

SMOKED AUBERGINE AND WALNUT DIP

MAKES A LARGE BOWL'S WORTH

2 fat aubergines (eggplants)
2 tbsp olive oil
2 tbsp pomegranate molasses
4 tbsp chopped walnuts
salt and pepper
a handful of pomegranate seeds
a few mint leaves, shredded

The crucial thing here is that you hold your nerve and really blacken the aubergine skin to get an intensely smoky flavour. If you can't find pomegranate molasses then substitute a good squeeze of lemon and a little honey.

UP TO 3 DAYS AHEAD (MIN. 2 HOURS):
Get the grill smoking hot. Prick the aubergines a few times with a fork and then put under the grill for 15–20 minutes, turning occasionally, until the skin is blackened and the flesh is soft. Alternatively, you can blacken the skins directly over a gas flame.

Put the aubergines in a bowl, cover with clingfilm and leave for 20 minutes, then peel and discard the skin. Blend or mash the flesh thoroughly with the olive oil and pomegranate molasses. Stir through the walnuts and season with salt and pepper to taste. Cover and chill.

1 HOUR AHEAD:
Take the dip out of the fridge (you don't want a cold dip).

TO SERVE:
Garnish with pomegranate seeds and shredded mint and serve.

ROASTED PEPPER AND ALMOND DIP

MAKES A LARGE BOWL'S WORTH

450–500g/about 1lb tomatoes, halved

salt and pepper

4 tbsp olive oil, plus a little more for the tomatoes

50g/1¾oz/⅓ cup blanched almonds

2 garlic cloves, sliced

250g/9oz roasted red peppers from a jar, drained

2 tbsp red wine vinegar

1 tsp chilli flakes

This is a romesco sauce of sorts, but one intended as a dip. I have absolutely no problem with cheating here and buying a jar of roasted red peppers, though if you prefer to roast your own, by all means do.

UP TO 3 DAYS AHEAD (MIN. 2 HOURS):

Get a grill good and hot. Season the tomatoes with salt and pepper and a little oil and pop under the grill for 10–15 minutes, until softened and lightly coloured.

Meanwhile, in a dry frying pan, toast the almonds until golden, taking care not to burn. Tip the almonds into a bowl. Add 2 tbsp olive oil to the pan and gently fry the garlic until lightly golden and soft.

Put the tomatoes, almonds, garlic, peppers, vinegar and chilli in a food processor with the remaining 2 tbsp olive oil. Season with a good pinch of salt and a twist of pepper and blend until smooth. Taste for seasoning and adjust with vinegar and/or salt, as necessary. Cover and chill.

30 MINUTES AHEAD:

Remove from the fridge. Gently warm before serving if you prefer.

BURNT ONION AND ANCHOVY SOUR CREAM

MAKES A LARGE BOWL'S WORTH

2 onions, halved, peeled and trimmed

salt and pepper

olive oil

4 anchovy fillets

1 small garlic clove, crushed to a paste

300ml/10fl oz/1¼ cups sour cream

a small bunch of chives

This works well as a crisp dip and/or something to dunk deep-fried goodies in.

UP TO 3 DAYS AHEAD (MIN. 2 HOURS):

Preheat the oven to 220°C/425°F/Gas mark 7. Season the onions with salt and pepper and rub with olive oil. Roast, cut side up, for 30 minutes, until blackened and soft. Blend in a food processor with the anchovy and garlic until smooth-ish. Leave to cool, then fold through the sour cream. Cover and chill.

TO SERVE:

Garnish with chopped chives and serve.

CHICKEN TIKKA WINGS WITH MINT YOGURT

15 whole chicken wings
2–4 red chillies, deseeded
     and finely chopped
1 garlic clove, crushed to
     a paste
1 tbsp grated fresh ginger
1 tbsp garam masala or good
     curry powder
2 tbsp tomato purée (paste)
juice of 1 lemon
2 tbsp vegetable oil
salt and pepper

For the mint yogurt
250g/9oz/1 cup plain yogurt
a handful of mint leaves,
     shredded
juice of ½ lemon
a pinch of ground cumin

To finish
fresh coriander (cilantro)

Not only *can* this be done well in advance, but the further ahead the better. The longer those wings get in the marinade, the more luscious they will be. You can jack up (or indeed down) the spice quotient as preferred.

UP TO 3 DAYS AHEAD (MIN. 4 HOURS):
Trim the wing tips off the wings and discard, or save for making stock (p.171). Cut the wings in half through the joints and place in a bowl.

In a food processor or pestle and mortar, blend the chillies, garlic, ginger, garam masala, tomato purée, lemon juice and oil until smooth. Add to the chicken along with a good pinch of salt and pepper, then cover and chill.

For the mint yogurt, mix all the ingredients in a small bowl, season with salt, cover and chill.

1¼ HOURS AHEAD:
Preheat the oven to 220°C/425°F/Gas mark 7. Tip the wings into an oiled baking tray. Roast for 15 minutes, then turn the oven down to 160°C/325°F/Gas mark 3. Cook for a further 45 minutes, shaking the tray now and then.

Take out of the oven and rest for 15 minutes.

TO SERVE
Garnish with coriander and serve with the mint yogurt.

CHEAT: Use a good-quality shop-bought tikka paste to marinate the chicken wings.
SCALING UP: Add ½ quantities of chilli and lemon juice each time you double.

HASSELBACK POTATOES WITH SOUR CREAM AND CAVIAR

MAKES 30
30 baby new potatoes
2 tbsp olive oil
salt and pepper
150ml/5½fl oz/⅔ cup sour
    cream
50g/1¾oz jar of lumpfish roe
sprigs of dill

These are a Swedish kind of roast spud. They look like the cook intended to slice the potatoes and then gave up, thus creating a great vehicle for all sorts of flavours.

UP TO 1 DAY AHEAD (MIN. 1 HOUR):
Preheat the oven to 200°C/400°F/Gas mark 6. Make 4–5 incisions in each potato about three quarters of the way through. Toss in olive oil, salt and pepper and then roast, cut side up, for 45 minutes, until crisp. Cool, cover and chill.

40 MINUTES AHEAD:
Preheat the oven to 200°C/400°F/Gas mark 6. Heat the potatoes for 15 minutes until hot and crisp. Garnish with a teaspoon of sour cream, a blob of lumpfish roe and a sprig of dill, and serve.

SCALING UP: Lumpfish roe goes quite a long way so you shouldn't need another jar.

PRAWN AND MANGO SALAD

MAKES ABOUT 20

3 red chillies, deseeded and
finely chopped

1 small mango, peeled,
stoned and finely diced

½ cucumber, peeled,
deseeded and finely diced

1 shallot, very finely chopped

20g/¾oz fresh coriander
(cilantro), chopped, plus
extra to garnish

2 tbsp fish sauce

juice of 3 limes

500g/1lb 2oz cooked
prawns (shrimp),
halved lengthways

20 baby gem lettuce leaves

A fresh and lively one that will go best with something sparkly rather than, say, mulled wine.

UP TO 1 DAY AHEAD (MIN. 20 MINUTES):

Mix the chillies, mango, cucumber, shallot, coriander, fish sauce and lime juice. Cover, and store in the fridge if making more than a couple of hours ahead.

15 MINUTES AHEAD:

Mix the prawns into the marinade. Spoon into the lettuce leaves. Garnish with coriander and serve.

SCALING UP: Go easy on the chillies, shallot and lime juice.

CHICKEN PASTILLA

25g/1oz/2 tbsp butter
1 onion, finely chopped
1 garlic clove, crushed to
    a paste
2 tbsp grated fresh ginger
salt and pepper
1 tsp ground cumin
1 tsp ground coriander
2 tsp ground cinnamon
4 chicken thighs
750ml/1¼ pints/3 cups
    chicken stock
100g/3½oz/1 cup ground
    almonds
3 tbsp runny honey
25g/1oz/¼ cup toasted flaked
    (slivered) almonds
25g/1oz/3 tbsp pistachios,
    roughly chopped
zest of 1 lemon
a good handful of parsley,
    finely chopped
8 sheets of filo pastry
100ml/3½fl oz/7 tbsp
    vegetable oil
1 egg, beaten
black sesame or
    mustard seeds

Pastilla is a North African pie traditionally made with squab pigeon. Its ingredients – cinnamon, almonds, honey, pastry – are pure Christmas. It's a lovely, evocative thing to have with your drinks. Serve with the roasted red pepper dip on p.41, or a good shop-bought salsa.

UP TO 3 DAYS AHEAD (MIN. 3 HOURS):

Melt the butter in a large saucepan over a low heat and add the onion, garlic and ginger. Season with salt and pepper, cover, and cook for 10–15 minutes, until soft. Turn up the heat slightly and add the cumin, coriander and cinnamon. Stir for a minute or so, then add the chicken thighs and stock. Bring to a boil and simmer gently for 1 hour, skimming off any scum that rises to the surface. Remove the thighs and cool.

Simmer the cooking liquor until reduced to about 200–250ml/ about 8fl oz/1 cup. Remove the chicken skin and discard along with the bones. Shred the meat and return to the pan with the ground almonds, honey, flaked almonds, pistachios, lemon zest and parsley. The mixture should be thick: if it's still a touch liquid, simmer until reduced. Taste for seasoning, then cool completely.

Take a sheet of filo and cut into 4 rectangles (keep the remaining sheets under a damp tea towel to prevent drying out). With each rectangle facing you vertically, brush with oil, then put a spoonful of filling crossways about 2.5cm/1in from the end nearest you. Brush the top end of the pastry with beaten egg, then roll into a cylinder. Transfer to a lightly floured baking sheet. Repeat until you have 32 pastry cigars. Chill for 20 minutes.

Preheat the oven to 180°C/350°F/Gas mark 4. Brush the outside of the pastries with beaten egg, sprinkle with sesame seeds, and bake for 25 minutes, until crisp. You may have to do this in batches. Cool on a wire rack, then chill or freeze.

TO REHEAT:

Preheat the oven to 200°C/400°F/Gas mark 6. Bake for 10 minutes from chilled, or 15 from frozen. Serve.

FREEZABLE

10 QUICK, QUIRKY PARTY FOOD CHEATS

- Olives are delicious. They're more delicious warm. Put them in a hot oven for a couple of minutes to accentuate those rich, fruity flavours.
- A big block of Parmesan, a cheese knife, oyster shucker, or garden trowel. Let guests hack off pieces of cheese. The perfect foil to a glass of Prosecco.
- Get a big jar of marinated artichokes, drape them in serrano or Parma ham, scatter with chopped parsley.
- Wrap breadsticks in Parma ham and serve with a good shop-bought pesto, or make your own (p.104).
- Shop-bought blinis, smoked salmon, sour cream, lumpfish caviar (the cheap stuff). Done in seconds and eaten even quicker.
- Scatter finely chopped parsley and a little olive oil over a plate of marinated anchovies.

QUICK TOAST TOPPINGS:
- Manchego cheese, quince jelly.
- Good-quality shop-bought pâté, caper berries.
- Rub with garlic, squish a tomato all over (then throw it away), finish with olive oil and sea salt.
- Get a block of lardo (cured pig fat) from an Italian deli. Roughly chop then blend with a drop of vinegar until smooth. Spread on toast.

CHRISTMAS EVE ETC

In many ways my favourite festive meals are the ones that straddle Christmas Day itself. These have all the cheer of the main event without the other distractions – and often there's no need to do everything in advance on these evenings. I love the buzz of putting dinner together while everyone bustles in and out of the kitchen, peeling a spud here, chopping an onion there – the cooking feels as much a part of dinner as the eating of it.

But sometimes cooking is the last thing you want to do. When you have guests turning up in need of attention, when the kids are going nuts from too much sugar and pre-Santa fever, when you need to wrap presents – these are not prime kitchen magic moments.

Then there's Boxing Day, when cooking is not likely to be high on your list of 'things I want to spend today doing', and New Year's Eve, which is far more enjoyable when you're not flapping around in the kitchen endeavouring to create something spectacular as midnight edges ever nearer.

This chapter is for those meals.

CHESTNUT AND CHORIZO SOUP WITH SAFFRON CREAM

SERVES 6–8

olive oil

200g/7oz chorizo, cut into
small cubes

1 onion, chopped

1 garlic clove, chopped

1 stick of celery, chopped

1 carrot, finely chopped

salt and pepper

½ tsp chilli flakes

1 tsp finely chopped rosemary

1 tsp ground cumin

200g/7oz cooked chestnuts,
roughly chopped

400g/14oz canned chopped
tomatoes

1 litre/1¾ pints/4 cups chicken
stock

100ml/3½fl oz/7 tbsp double
(heavy) cream

a few saffron strands

This was inspired by a dish in the first *Moro* cookbook by Sam and Sam Clark, a beauty that should be on any vaguely keen cook's shelf. Their soup is somewhat chunkier than this one. Either way, it's a cracker – gently spiced, aromatic, velvety, entirely Christmassy. And will only improve from being made some days in advance.

UP TO 3 DAYS AHEAD (MIN. 1 HOUR):

Heat a drop of oil in a large saucepan and fry the chorizo until crisp. Remove with a slotted spoon and set aside. Add the onion, garlic, celery and carrot to the pan. Season with salt and pepper and cook over a low heat for 15–20 minutes, until soft and lightly golden. Add the chilli flakes, rosemary and cumin and stir for a minute or so, then add the chestnuts, tomatoes, stock, and half the chorizo. Bring to a boil and simmer gently for 15 minutes. Blend until smooth, leave to cool, then chill or freeze.

In a small pan, gently warm the cream with the saffron for 5 minutes, then set aside to cool. Cover and chill.

30 MINUTES AHEAD:

Warm the soup over a gentle heat, stirring occasionally. Take the saffron cream out of the fridge. Put the remaining chorizo in a warm oven or gently warm through in a frying pan. Warm some bowls if possible (I never remember).

TO SERVE:

Ladle into bowls and top with a few chunks of chorizo and a dribble of saffron cream.

FREEZABLE (without saffron cream)

PICKLED HERRING AND SPICED ONION ON RYE

SERVES 6

2 shallots, thinly sliced

1 bay leaf

10 juniper berries,
    lightly crushed

100ml/3½fl oz/7 tbsp vodka

500ml/18fl oz/generous 2 cups
    cider vinegar

2 tbsp salt

1 tbsp sugar

2 tbsp chopped dill

6 herring, gutted and filleted

For the spiced onion

100g/3½oz/½ cup caster
    (superfine) sugar

150ml/5fl oz/⅔ cup white wine
    vinegar

1 tbsp coriander seeds,
    crushed

1 tsp cumin seeds, crushed

1 tsp fennel seeds, crushed

1 clove

1 tsp salt

1 large red onion, peeled
    whole and sliced
    into rounds

To serve

rye bread, sliced

butter

sprigs of dill

If you do one thing this Christmas, make some pickled herring. A big, glistening jar of this in the fridge will be a great ally at this time of year – handy for quick canapés, acceptable as a present, ideal for starters like this. If you can't get hold of herring, mackerel is a good alternative.

UP TO 1 WEEK AHEAD (MIN. 6 HOURS):

Put the shallots, bay leaf, juniper, vodka, vinegar, salt and sugar in a saucepan and bring to a boil, stirring to dissolve the sugar and salt. Simmer for 3 minutes, take off the heat and leave until cool. Tip into a large sterilized jar (see note on p.200) or non-metallic dish. Add the dill and herring, making sure the fish is submerged. Cover and chill in the fridge.

For the spiced onion: put the sugar, vinegar, spices and salt in a pan and bring to a boil, stirring to dissolve. Simmer for 3 minutes, then tip over the onion in a non-metallic dish. Cover and store in a cool, dry place until needed.

TO SERVE:

Toast the rye bread, if preferred, and spread with butter. Top with pickled herring and spiced onion, garnish with a few dill sprigs and serve.

SCALING UP: If doubling the recipe, no need to double shallots or bay leaf.

FISH SOUP WITH CROUTONS, GRUYÈRE AND ROUILLE

SERVES 6–8

2 tbsp olive oil

1 onion, finely sliced

1 stick celery, finely chopped

1 fennel bulb, thinly sliced

salt and pepper

1 garlic clove, thinly sliced

½ tsp fennel seeds, crushed

a few peppercorns

400g/14oz canned chopped
    tomatoes

1 strip of orange peel

½ tsp chilli flakes

a few saffron strands

500g/1lb 2oz fish trimmings
    and bones, washed,
    or 1.5 litres/2½ pints/
    generous 6 cups fish stock

1.5 litres/2½ pints/generous
    6 cups water (unless using
    ready-made fish stock)

150ml/5fl oz/⅔ cup dry white
    wine or vermouth

500g/1lb 2oz skinless white
    fish, cut into chunks

For the rouille

2 slices of cooked red pepper,
    from a jar

2 tbsp tomato purée (paste)

½ tsp cayenne pepper

2 egg yolks

1 garlic clove, crushed

100ml/3½fl oz/7 tbsp olive oil

juice of ½ lemon

To serve

olive oil

2 long baguettes, thinly sliced

50g/1¾oz Gruyère cheese

No innovation here – just a rich and deeply flavoured soup as served in the south of France, with crisp croutons, grated cheese and a spoonful of garlicky red pepper sauce. Ask your fishmonger for bones and trimmings from white fish, or pick up some ready-made fish stock. You can make this well in advance (up to a month) and freeze the soup, if necessary.

UP TO 1 DAY AHEAD (MIN. 2 HOURS):

Heat the oil in a large pan over a low heat and add the onion, celery and fennel. Season with salt and pepper, cover and cook gently for 20 minutes until soft, taking care not to colour. Add the garlic, fennel seeds and peppercorns and stir for a minute or so, then add the tomatoes, orange peel, chilli flakes, saffron, fish trimmings and water (or fish stock) and wine. Bring to a boil and simmer very gently for 1 hour.

Remove the orange peel and fish bones if necessary, and add the fish. Simmer for 10 minutes, then blend until smooth. Pass through a sieve into a clean pan. Taste for seasoning and adjust if necessary. Cool and chill, or freeze.

To make the rouille, put the red pepper, tomato purée, cayenne, egg yolks and garlic in a small food processor along with a pinch of salt and blend until smooth. Continue to blend, adding the oil a little at a time, until it comes together. Add the lemon juice, spoon into a bowl, cover and chill.

30 MINUTES AHEAD:

Put the soup over a gentle heat to warm through, stirring from time to time. Warm some bowls in a low oven if possible.

Heat a little oil in a large frying pan and fry the baguette slices with a pinch of salt for a couple of minutes on each side until golden. Set aside. Grate the Gruyère cheese.

TO SERVE:

Ladle soup into bowls. Garnish with croutons, Gruyère and rouille.

FREEZABLE (soup)

SCALING UP: Extra fish trimmings unnecessary for the stock. 2 egg yolks will be plenty in the rouille even when scaled up.

CHICKEN LIVER PÂTÉ WITH PICKLED GRAPES

SERVES 6

250g/9oz/generous 1 cup
   unsalted butter, softened
1 tbsp olive oil
400g/14oz chicken livers,
   trimmed of any green or
   stringy bits
salt and pepper
2 shallots, finely chopped
1 garlic clove, sliced
2 tsp chopped thyme
100ml/3½fl oz/7 tbsp brandy

For the pickled grapes

50g/1¾oz/¼ cup caster
   (superfine) sugar
200ml/7fl oz/generous ¾ cup
   vinegar
1 bay leaf
½ tsp salt
300g/10½oz red grapes
1 shallot, finely sliced

To serve

toast
butter

CHEAT: Instead of pickled
grapes, serve with shop-
bought cornichons (mini
pickled gherkins).
SCALING UP: No need to
whack a load of bay leaves
into the pickle – one will
be plenty.

A festive starter that might just as well be served as nibbles for a bigger party. Pickled grapes perhaps sound mildly bizarre but they're a good foil to the rich, buttery pâté. All of this can be done well in advance. Store in individual pots or in one serving dish.

UP TO 3 DAYS AHEAD (MIN. 6 HOURS):

Melt half the butter over a very low heat until the milk solids separate to the bottom. Carefully tip the clarified top layer into a jug and set aside. Keep the milk solids for the pâté.

In a large frying pan, heat the olive oil over a medium heat and fry the livers for a couple of minutes on each side, seasoning with salt and pepper, until browned. Remove and set aside, then add the shallots and garlic and cook over a gentle heat for 15 minutes, until softened. Return the liver to the pan along with the thyme and cook for a further 3 minutes. Whack up the heat and add the brandy. Boil hard for 30 seconds or so, then reduce the heat and simmer for 2 minutes.

Transfer to a food processor with the remaining butter and the milk solids, and blend until smooth. Taste for seasoning and adjust if necessary. Scoop into a serving bowl or individual pots, pat flat, and pour over the clarified butter. Once cool, cover and chill in the fridge.

For the pickled grapes: mix the sugar and vinegar until dissolved, then add the bay leaf and salt. Halve the grapes (peel if you prefer, but it's a fairly time-consuming job) and add to the vinegar along with the shallot. Store in a cool place.

1 HOUR AHEAD:

Take the pâté out of the fridge.

10 MINUTES AHEAD:

Make some toast.

TO SERVE:

Serve the pâté with pickled grapes, toast and butter.

COFFEE-ROASTED BEETROOT WITH HORSERADISH AND BUTTERMILK DRESSING AND TOASTED HAZELNUTS

SERVES 6

500g/1lb 2oz coffee beans
(nothing fancy)
750g/1lb 10oz beetroot,
washed but not peeled
50g/1¾oz/scant ½ cup
blanched hazelnuts,
roughly chopped
3 tbsp freshly grated
horseradish (or grated
horseradish from a jar)
3 tbsp buttermilk or
sour cream
2 tbsp white wine vinegar
salt and pepper
6 tbsp olive oil
100g/3½oz mixed salad
leaves

Roasting root vegetables in coffee might sound bizarre, but it tastes sensational, accentuating the sweetness of the root and adding wonderfully evocative coffee notes. Once you've tried it, you'll do it again and again.

UP TO 3 DAYS AHEAD (MIN. 2 HOURS):

Preheat the oven to 200°C/400°F/Gas mark 6. Tip the coffee beans into a roasting pan and top with the beetroot. Cover tightly with a couple of layers of foil and roast for 1 hour. Remove from the oven and leave to cool, then rub the skins off the beetroot with your thumb. Quarter, cover and store in a cool place until needed. Discard the coffee beans.

Meanwhile, heat a dry frying pan over a medium heat and add the hazelnuts. Toast, shaking the pan regularly, until golden and aromatic. Set aside.

To make the dressing, mix the horseradish, buttermilk and vinegar with a good pinch of salt and pepper, then whisk in the olive oil. Store in a bowl or jar in the fridge.

1 HOUR AHEAD:

Take the beetroot and dressing out of the fridge if necessary.

TO SERVE:

Toss the hazelnuts through the salad leaves. Top with beetroot and spoon over the dressing.

CHEAT: Use cooked beetroot – make sure it's not vinegared. Add a pinch of ground coffee to the dressing.
SCALING UP: If roasting more beetroot there's no need to use more coffee than this.

VENISON WELLINGTON WITH ROAST ONIONS AND ÉPOISSES CHEESE

SERVES 6–8

about 1kg/2lb 4oz venison loin

25g/1oz/2 tbsp unsalted butter

2 shallots, finely chopped

2 garlic cloves, finely chopped

1 tsp chopped thyme

200g/7oz button mushrooms, sliced

salt and pepper

100ml/3½fl oz/7 tbsp Marsala or Madeira

a good handful of parsley, finely chopped

375g/13oz puff pastry

1 egg, beaten

For the roast onions

3–4 onions, quartered

2 tbsp olive oil

100g/3½oz Époisses cheese, or Camembert, sliced and stored in the fridge

For the gravy

50g/1¾oz/4 tbsp unsalted butter

2 shallots, sliced

1 garlic clove, squished with the flat of a knife

a sprig of thyme

250ml/9fl oz/generous 1 cup red wine

250ml/9fl oz/generous 1 cup beef stock

2 tbsp balsamic vinegar

50g/1¾oz/4 tbsp cold butter, cubed

This is a treat, a New Year's Eve dish, and very much one for the grown-ups. If you find beef fillet too politely flavoured then this venison may be the way forward.

UP TO 1 DAY AHEAD (MIN. 2 HOURS):

Get a big frying pan good and hot and brown the venison all over. Remove to a plate and set aside to cool.

Add the butter to the same pan and gently fry the shallots until soft. Add the garlic, thyme and mushrooms, season with salt and pepper, and cook for a few minutes until softened. Add the Marsala and any juices that have come out of the meat, and simmer until reduced and sticky. Stir through the parsley, then set aside to cool completely.

Roll out the pastry into a long rectangle about 3mm/⅛in thick. Top with the mushrooms, leaving a 2.5cm/1in border around the outside. Lay the venison down the middle and season with salt and pepper. Brush the border with beaten egg, then roll tightly around the venison, sealing the edges. Turn over so the join is underneath and mark a very light criss-cross pattern on the pastry, using the blunt side of a knife. Transfer to a lightly floured baking sheet, seam side down, cover with clingfilm and chill in the fridge.

To make the gravy, melt the butter over a medium heat then add the shallots, season with salt and pepper, and cook for a few minutes until softened and golden. Add the garlic, thyme and red wine. Bring to a boil and simmer to reduce by half. Add the stock and bring back to a boil. Simmer for 20 minutes, stir in the vinegar, and taste for seasoning. Strain through a sieve, cool, then cover and chill.

1¼ HOURS AHEAD:

Preheat the oven to 200°C/400°F/Gas mark 6.

Brush the pastry with beaten egg. Toss the onions in the olive oil with salt and pepper. Roast the onions for 15 minutes, then add the venison to the oven and cook for 30–40 minutes, until the pastry is golden. Remove both the venison and the onions from the oven. Leave the venison to rest in a warm place.

CHEAT: Instead of the mushroom stuffing, use a good quality shop-bought tapenade.

Lay the cheese over the onions and return to the oven for 5 minutes to melt.

Warm the gravy up to a gentle simmering point, then whisk in the butter. Keep warm over a gentle heat.

TO SERVE:

Slice the wellington thickly and serve with the cheesy roast onions and a good spoonful of gravy.

GUINNESS AND MARMALADE HAM WITH CELERIAC DAUPHINOIS

SERVES 6–8

2.5–3kg/5–6½lb unsmoked
   boneless gammon
1 litre/1¾ pints/4 cups stout
1 onion, halved (don't peel)
a bulb of garlic, halved
   horizontally
1 bay leaf
1 tbsp peppercorns
1 leek, roughly chopped
1 carrot, roughly chopped

For the glaze
3 tbsp marmalade
3 tbsp English mustard
   powder, mixed with
   2 tbsp water
3 tbsp olive oil
½ tsp ground cloves
salt and pepper

For the dauphinois
20g/¾oz/1½ tbsp butter,
   softened
1kg/2lb 4oz celeriac, peeled
2 red chillies, deseeded and
   finely chopped
500ml/18fl oz/generous 2 cups
   double (heavy) cream
25g/1oz Gruyère cheese,
   grated

FREEZABLE
SCALING UP: Don't go
nuts with the chillies in
the dauphinois. Bay leaf,
peppercorns etc in the ham
stock don't need doubling.

For certain of us Brits, Boxing Day means one thing – ham. A big, ruddy ham for the whole family and any hangers-on to pile into. Its satellites are, more often than not, leftovers from Christmas lunch, but there's no reason not to make a little extra. I think creamy dauphinois potatoes work beautifully, though here I've changed it in favour of celeriac with a kick of chilli.

UP TO 3 DAYS AHEAD (MIN. 4 HOURS):
The ham is likely to be salty. Combat this by putting it in a pan and adding fresh water to cover; bring to a boil, then chuck out the water and start again with the stout and enough fresh water to cover the ham. Add the onion, garlic, bay leaf, peppercorns, leek and carrot. Bring to a boil and simmer very gently, uncovered, for 2 hours, skimming off any scum on the surface. Remove from the liquid and leave to cool, then peel off the skin and discard.

For the glaze, mix the marmalade, mustard, olive oil and ground cloves and season with salt and pepper. Score the ham fat in a criss-cross pattern and rub the glaze all over. Cover and chill in the fridge. Or freeze.

For the dauphinois, preheat oven to 180°C/350°F/Gas mark 4. Rub a baking dish with a little butter. Cut the celeriac into quarters, then slice thinly. Layer this up in the baking dish with the chillies, salt, pepper, and cream. Finish with a sprinkling of cheese. Bake for 1 hour. Serve, or cool, then cover and chill if necessary. Or freeze.

90 MINUTES AHEAD:
Preheat the oven to 200°C/400°F/Gas mark 6. Bake the ham for 1 hour. If the glaze starts to catch, cover loosely with foil.

30 MINUTES AHEAD:
Reheat the celeriac dauphinois in the hot oven.

15 MINUTES AHEAD:
Take the ham out of the oven and rest.

TO SERVE:
Carve the ham and serve with the celeriac dauphinois.

FISH PIE

SERVES 6–8

125g/4½oz/generous ½ cup
   unsalted butter
1 onion, finely chopped
1 garlic clove, sliced
salt and pepper
150ml/5fl oz/⅔ cup dry white
   wine
750ml/1¼ pints/3 cups whole
   milk
bay leaf, thyme sprigs and
   parsley stalks, tied into a
   bouquet garni
600g/1lb 5oz white fish,
   skinned and cubed
300g/10½oz smoked
   haddock, skinned
   and cubed
300g/10½oz raw king prawns
   (shrimp)
25g/1oz/3 tbsp plain
   (all-purpose) flour
a good handful of parsley,
   finely chopped
1kg/2lb 4oz floury potatoes,
   such as Maris Piper, King
   Edward or Desiree

At this time of year there will almost inevitably be an evening when the thought of cooking is about the least appealing thing you can imagine. Having a good fish pie tucked away in the freezer will be an enormous relief on such days. This version is gussied up only slightly by the addition of prawns, but is otherwise as trad as it gets.

UP TO 2 DAYS AHEAD (MIN. 3 HOURS):

Melt 25g/1oz/2 tbsp of the butter in a large saucepan. Add the onion and garlic, season with salt and pepper, cover and cook over a gentle heat for 15 minutes or so until soft. Add the wine, whack up the heat and simmer for a few minutes. Add 600ml/20fl oz/2½ cups milk and the bunch of herbs, reduce the heat and simmer very gently for 20 minutes.

Add the fish and prawns and poach for 5–7 minutes, until the prawns have changed colour, then remove with a slotted spoon. Soften 25g/1oz/2 tbsp of the butter in a small bowl and beat together with the flour, then add to the cooking liquor, whisking to dissolve. Continue to simmer until the sauce is thicker than you perhaps feel is right – it'll loosen up when you return the fish to the pan. Remove the bunch of herbs, and add the chopped parsley and fish. Season with salt and pepper to taste. Tip into a buttered baking dish and leave to cool.

Meanwhile, peel the potatoes and cut into quarters, then bring to a boil in a pan of salted water. Simmer for 20–25 minutes, until softened, then drain and mash with the remaining butter and milk, and plenty of salt and pepper. Leave until completely cool, then spread over the fish and chill or freeze.

1 HOUR AHEAD:

Preheat the oven to 200°C/400°F/Gas mark 6. Bake the fish pie for 35–40 minutes, until golden.

TO SERVE:

I love fish pie with peas and, gulp, tomato ketchup.

FREEZABLE

CHEAT: There's nothing wrong with ready-chopped fish pie mix.

ROAST DUCK WITH BLACKBERRIES

SERVES 4–6

2kg/4lb 8oz duck, ideally
    including giblets
25g/1oz/2 tbsp butter
4 shallots, sliced
2 garlic cloves, sliced
1 stick of celery, chopped
salt and pepper
300ml/10fl oz/1¼ cups red
    wine
300ml/10fl oz/1¼ cups
    chicken stock
a big sprig of thyme
1 bay leaf
25g/1oz/2 tbsp cold butter,
    cubed
3 tbsp balsamic vinegar
200g/7oz blackberries

A roast duck is one of the table's great treats. Skin crisp and quietly singing, flesh juicy and rich, it is up there with beef fillet for pure indulgence. Blackberries provide a nice acidic edge as a foil to the fatty duck.

120°C might seem an inordinately low temperature to 'roast' something at, but it means the bird just slowly ticks over for a few hours, leaving you to get on with other things.

UP TO 1 DAY AHEAD (MIN. 5 HOURS):

Cut the wing tips off the duck. Discard the liver (or save for something like the terrine on p.90), then roughly chop the remaining giblets. Melt the butter over a medium–high heat in a wide pan and add the giblets, wing tips, shallots, garlic and celery. Season with salt and pepper and cook for 10 minutes or so, stirring regularly, until golden and softened. Add the wine, bring to a boil, then gently simmer to reduce by half. Add the stock and herbs, simmer gently for 30 minutes, then strain through a sieve. Leave to cool, cover, and chill.

3½ HOURS AHEAD:

Preheat the oven to 120°C/250°F/Gas mark ½. Prick the duck very lightly all over with a needle, taking care not to pierce through to the flesh. Rub all over with salt and pepper, then place in a roasting pan and cook for 2 hours. Remove from the oven and tip away the excess fat (save it for roast potatoes). Whack up the oven to 220°C/425°F/Gas mark 7 and return the duck to the oven. Roast for a further 30–45 minutes, until the skin is crisp.

30 MINUTES AHEAD:

Gently warm the gravy.

Remove the duck from the oven and transfer to a plate (ideally warmed), and rest in a warm place. Tip any additional excess fat from the pan. Put the roasting pan over a medium–high heat and add a splash of water. Simmer, scraping up all the caramelized juices stuck in the pan, then tip these into the gravy. Bring the gravy up to a simmer and add the cubed butter, whisking well. Add the balsamic vinegar and blackberries, taste for seasoning and add a little salt if necessary. Keep warm.

TO SERVE:
Carve the duck and serve with the blackberry gravy.

SCALING UP: If cooking a larger duck, give it another 30 minutes per 500g. For more gravy, add extra stock and reduce, tasting as you go.

HERB-STUFFED LEG OF LAMB WITH WATERCRESS AND ANCHOVY SAUCE

50g/1¾oz parsley leaves (the odd stalk is fine)

10g/¼oz mint leaves

2 tbsp rosemary needles, roughly chopped

2 garlic cloves, roughly chopped

4 tbsp olive oil

1 boned leg of lamb, about 2kg/4lb 8oz

salt and pepper

For the sauce

200g/7oz watercress

25g/1oz parsley

50g/1¾oz canned anchovies

100g/3½oz/7 tbsp unsalted butter

juice of ½ lemon

I've cooked this dish perhaps more than any other recipe in this book – it's something I roll out on any occasion, given half a chance. I love its relative simplicity, the ease of carving it, and how handsome and vivid the stuffing and sauce look on the plate.

UP TO 3 DAYS AHEAD (MIN. 2 HOURS):

Put the parsley, mint, rosemary, garlic and olive oil in a blender with a good pinch of salt and pepper and blend until smooth. Alternatively finely chop the herbs and garlic and mix with the oil.

Lay the lamb fat-side down on a board and season. Spread the herb mix across the inside, roll up tightly, then tie up tightly with string (there are videos online to guide). Cover and chill.

UP TO 1 DAY AHEAD (MIN. 1 HOUR):

To make the sauce, get a pan of salted water on the boil, and fill a bowl with ice-cold water. Add the watercress and parsley to the boiling water and leave for 30 seconds, then transfer to the iced water. Leave to cool, drain, then squeeze out all the liquid. Finely chop or blend in a food processor, together with the anchovies, then cover and chill.

2 HOURS AHEAD:

Preheat the oven to 220°C/425°F/Gas mark 7. Take the lamb out of the fridge and season all over with salt and pepper.

90 MINUTES AHEAD:

Roast the lamb for 15 minutes, then turn the oven down to 190°C/375°F/Gas mark 5 and roast for a further 45 minutes. Remove from the oven, cover loosely with foil and rest in a warm place.

15 MINUTES AHEAD:

To finish the sauce, melt the butter over a medium heat and add the watercress/anchovy mixture. Gently simmer for a few minutes, stirring occasionally, then stir in lemon juice and a twist of pepper.

TO SERVE:

Carve the lamb in thick slices and serve with the sauce on the side.

SPICE-CRUSTED MONKFISH WITH SWEETCORN FRITTERS AND HERB YOGURT

SERVES 6

1 tbsp coriander seeds

1 tsp cumin seeds

1 tsp fennel seeds

½ tsp peppercorns

seeds from 5 cardamom pods

5 cloves

1 tsp ground turmeric

6 x 200g/7oz pieces monkfish

1 tbsp vegetable oil

For the herb yogurt

300g/10½oz/1¼ cups plain yogurt

25g/1oz fresh coriander (cilantro), finely chopped

20 mint leaves, finely chopped

a small bunch of chives, finely chopped

juice of 1 lime

a pinch of salt

For the sweetcorn fritters

about 300g/10½oz canned sweetcorn, drained

1 green chilli, deseeded and finely chopped

2 spring onions (scallions), finely chopped

85g/3oz/scant ¾ cup self-raising flour

a pinch of salt

a pinch of sugar

2 eggs

100ml/3½fl oz/7 tbsp milk

2 tbsp vegetable oil

To serve

lime wedges

fresh coriander (cilantro)

Fish is a tricky one to fit under the do-ahead umbrella, not taking kindly, on the whole, to sitting around after being cooked. You can get ahead in other ways, however, by getting the side bits and pieces done so all you need to do is bung the fish in the oven.

UP TO 1 DAY AHEAD (MIN. 2 HOURS):

In a dry frying pan, toast the whole spices until fragrant, taking care not to burn. Grind in a pestle and mortar or grinder until fine, then add the turmeric. Toss the monkfish in the spice mix and chill.

To make the herb yogurt, stir the herbs through the yogurt with the lime juice and a good pinch of salt. Cover and chill.

For the fritters, mix the sweetcorn, chilli and spring onions in a bowl. In a separate bowl, mix the flour, salt and sugar. In a third bowl whisk together the eggs and milk, then add to the flour, whisking until all the lumps have gone. Add to the sweetcorn until coated but not too wet (you may not need all the mixture). Rest for 20 minutes.

Heat the oil in a heavy frying pan and add spoonfuls of the sweetcorn batter. Fry over a medium–high heat for a couple of minutes on each side until crisp and golden (in batches if necessary), then set aside on kitchen paper. If you're proceeding to dinner, keep warm, otherwise cool and chill, or freeze.

45 MINUTES AHEAD:

Take the monkfish out of the fridge and season with a good pinch of salt. Preheat the oven to 200°C/400°F/Gas mark 6.

20 MINUTES AHEAD:

Heat a tablespoon of oil in an ovenproof frying pan and fry the monkfish for a couple of minutes on each side, until browned. Transfer to the oven along with the sweetcorn fritters, and roast for 10–12 minutes, until firm to the touch.

TO SERVE:

Plate the monkfish with the sweetcorn fritters and a dollop of herb yogurt. Garnish with lime wedges and coriander, and serve.

FREEZABLE (fritters)

ROAST ONION, POTATO AND BLUE CHEESE PIE

SERVES 4–6

3 onions, quartered

1 tsp chopped thyme

4–5 tbsp olive oil

salt and pepper

500g/1lb 2oz new potatoes

7 sheets of filo pastry

a good handful of parsley,
   finely chopped

200g/7oz blue cheese,
   roughly chopped

A lovely vegetarian main with a festive feel. Serve with a salad of parsley and capers.

UP TO 3 DAYS AHEAD (MIN. 3 HOURS):

Preheat the oven to 200°C/400°F/Gas mark 6. Toss the quartered onions with the thyme, a glug of oil and a good pinch of salt and pepper. Roast in the oven for 45 minutes until nicely coloured (I like them a little blackened). Cool.

Meanwhile, cut the potatoes into smallish pieces and bring to a boil in a pan of salted water. Simmer for 8–10 minutes, until tender. Drain and cool.

Lay a sheet of filo pastry in a 20cm/8in tart or cake tin and brush with olive oil. Lay another sheet on top at 90 degrees and brush with oil. Repeat with three more sheets of filo, placing each at 45 degrees to the previous one. Toss together the onions, potatoes, parsley and blue cheese, and fill the tart with them. Brush the last two sheets of filo with oil and cut each into four. Scrunch up and top the pie with them. Bake in the oven for 20 minutes, until golden and crisp. Serve warm or leave to cool, then cover and chill or freeze.

45 MINUTES AHEAD:

Preheat the oven to 200°C/400°F/Gas mark 6. Reheat the pie for 20 minutes, then keep warm until ready to serve.

TO SERVE:

Hack the pie into slices and serve.

FREEZABLE

SPICED AUBERGINE STEW WITH PARSLEY AND PISTACHIOS

4 tbsp olive oil

4 onions, thinly sliced

4 large aubergines
(eggplants), quartered
lengthways

salt and pepper

2 garlic cloves,
finely chopped

2 tsp ground coriander

1 tsp ground cumin

½ tsp sweet smoked paprika

½ tsp chilli flakes

1 cinnamon stick

2 x 400g/14oz cans chopped
tomatoes

1 tsp sugar

25g/1oz parsley leaves

2 tbsp dill fronds

25g/1oz shelled pistachios,
roughly chopped

2 tsp red wine vinegar

2 tbsp olive oil

It has become something of a running joke between my supper club partner Sam and me that vegetarian guests are always fed aubergine. This isn't strictly fair, though there's a kernel of truth in it – I love aubergines and when I'm having a meat-free day they're one of the most satisfying things to eat, thus they're what I like to feed our non-meat-eating guests.

As with most stews, this will benefit from being made a day or two in advance. Serve with rice or couscous and a dollop of yogurt.

UP TO 3 DAYS AHEAD (MIN. 90 MINUTES):

Heat half the oil in a large pan, add the onions and fry over a medium–low heat, stirring occasionally, for 30–40 minutes, until soft and golden. Meanwhile, heat the remaining oil in a non-stick frying pan and fry the aubergine, a few pieces at a time, until browned, seasoning with salt and pepper as you go (you may need to add a little more oil). Add the garlic and spices to the onions and stir for a minute or so, then add the aubergine to this pan along with the tomatoes and sugar. Cover and simmer gently for 30 minutes. Taste for seasoning, then set aside to cool. Cover and chill, or freeze.

30 MINUTES AHEAD:

Reheat the stew over a gentle heat. Toss the parsley, dill and pistachios together with the vinegar, olive oil, and a pinch of salt.

TO SERVE:

Serve the stew with the parsley and pistachio garnish.

FREEZABLE

CHEAT: I'm rather fond of canned aubergines, which you can find in most ethnic stores. They tend to be quite oily, so pour off any excess.

SCALING UP: Go easy on the oil and the onions. You'll only need 1 cinnamon stick.

TANGERINE GRANITA

SERVES 8
20 tangerines
juice of 1 lemon
100g/3½oz/¾ cup icing
   (confectioners') sugar

A granita is a sorbet that grew up on the rough side of town. Instead of being gently churned during the freezing, it freezes hard, only to be frisked by a fork before it's too late. This is what creates the pleasing, shard-like texture of a granita, as opposed to the smooth texture of sorbet. If you'd prefer to use an ice-cream machine to make a sorbet, then do.

UP TO 1 WEEK AHEAD (MIN. 6 HOURS):
Zest half the tangerines, taking care not to grate the white pith, which will make the granita bitter. Juice all of them and combine with the lemon juice and sugar. Taste and add a little more sugar if necessary (it should be slightly more sweet than you want – the freezing mutes the sugar a little). Tip into a bowl or plastic container and freeze for 6 hours. Whisk thoroughly with a fork to mash up into shards, and return to the freezer until needed.

TO SERVE:
Remove the granita from the freezer and give it another good whisk with a fork before serving.

APPLE SNOW WITH FENNEL BISCUITS

SERVES 6

For the fennel biscuits

100g/3½oz/7 tbsp unsalted butter, softened

100g/3½oz/½ cup caster (superfine) sugar

a pinch of sea salt

1 tsp fennel seeds, lightly crushed

zest of 1 lemon

150g/5½oz/1¼ cups plain (all-purpose) flour

For the apple snow

2 large cooking apples (500–600g/about 1¼lb)

juice of 1 lemon

150g/5½oz/¾ cup caster (superfine) sugar

2 egg whites

To serve

double (heavy) cream

I'd forgotten entirely about apple snow until I was served it at a party in Wales, triggering Proustian memories of me, graze-kneed and dangle-legged, eating it as a small boy. To my 28-year-old self it was every bit as delightful as it had been when I was little.

UP TO 1 WEEK AHEAD (MIN. 2 HOURS):

Make the fennel biscuits: beat the butter, sugar, salt, fennel seeds and lemon zest together until pale and light. Sift in the flour a little at a time, stirring as you go, until it forms a dough. Knead briefly with lightly floured hands until it comes together.

Roll out the dough on a lightly floured surface to about 1cm/½in thick, and cut out 12 biscuits. Prick a few times with a fork, then put on a baking sheet and chill for 20–30 minutes.

Preheat the oven to 160°C/325°F/Gas mark 3. Bake the biscuits for 15–20 minutes until pale golden. Transfer to a wire rack to cool. Store in an airtight container in a cool, dry place.

UP TO 1 DAY AHEAD (MIN. 2 HOURS):

Peel, core and roughly chop the apples. Put in a pan with the lemon juice, sugar, and a splash of water. Cover and cook over a medium–low heat for 10–15 minutes, stirring regularly, until completely softened. Blend until smooth, then transfer to a bowl and leave to cool. In a clean bowl, whisk the egg whites until they form stiff peaks. Fold the whites thoroughly, though gently, through the cold apple, then cover and chill.

TO SERVE:

Serve the apple snow with the biscuits and a splash of cream.

FREEZABLE (BISCUITS)

CHEAT: Serve with shop-bought shortbread or almond thins.

CHOCOLATE, ORANGE AND HAZELNUT TART

SERVES 6–8 (10–12 AT A PUSH)

For the pastry

100g/3½oz/7 tbsp cold butter, cubed

200g/7oz/generous 1½ cups plain (all-purpose) flour

a pinch of salt

2 eggs

For the filling

300ml/10fl oz/1¼ cups double (heavy) cream

300g/10½oz dark chocolate, broken into pieces

1 egg and 2 egg yolks

100g/3½oz/½ cup caster (superfine) sugar

100g/3½oz/¾ cup hazelnuts, toasted, then chopped

zest of 1 orange

To serve

icing (confectioners') sugar

single (light) cream

I was tempted to remove the comma from the title of this recipe, and make it using a well-known cricket ball-sized confection. Perhaps it's for the best that I didn't. This is a treat.

UP TO 3 DAYS AHEAD (MIN. 3 HOURS):

To make the pastry, rub the butter into the flour until it resembles breadcrumbs (I usually pulse in the food processor). Add the salt and then one of the eggs and mix until it forms a dough. Add a little cold water if it isn't coming together. Briefly knead, wrap in clingfilm and chill in the freezer for 10 minutes, or the fridge for 30 minutes.

On a lightly floured work surface, roll out the dough to about 3mm/⅛in thick. Line a 25cm/10in tart tin, prick a few times with a fork, and return to the fridge for 30 minutes. Meanwhile, preheat the oven to 160°C/325°F/Gas mark 3.

Line the pastry with baking parchment and fill with baking beans, dried chickpeas or old pasta – anything to weigh it down. Bake for 25–30 minutes until golden. Remove the baking beans and parchment. Beat the remaining egg and brush the pastry all over. Return to the oven and bake for another 5 minutes, then remove and leave to cool. Turn the oven down to 150° C/300°F/ Gas mark 2.

Meanwhile, make the filling. Slowly bring the cream to a boil, then take off the heat and add the chocolate pieces. Stir, then leave to melt completely. In a bowl, beat the eggs and sugar until pale and fluffy, then beat this mixture into the melted chocolate. Fold through the hazelnuts and orange zest. Tip into the tart shell and bake in the oven for 20 minutes. Leave to cool completely, cover and chill or freeze.

TO SERVE:

Dust with icing sugar and serve the tart with single cream.

FREEZABLE

CHEAT: Use shop-bought shortcrust pastry, or a good-quality pastry shell.

CHRISTMAS DAY

And so we arrive at Christmas Day and the Christmas meal. Whether this is lunch, dinner, or somewhere in between falls to each family's own rituals, though odds are it will be a quite unnecessarily – and yet oddly completely necessary – large meal. Any notion of meat-and-two-veg goes sailing out the window as we spoon roast potato after sprout after carrot after stuffing onto our groaning plates. On no other day would such lily-gilding work and yet on this day it just does.

This means there is much to do. But – guess what – you can do pretty much all of it a day or two in advance, some things even longer. Sauces, spuds, stuffings and so on can all have their boxes ticked before Santa's lardy rear has touched its sleigh. That's not to say these jobs are all 5-minuters – you're not going to pull a meal of these proportions together with a Jamie Oliver-style wave of the wand – but the fact that you can get them done in the run-up to Christmas Day means that, on the day, you'll be as cool as a Canadian cucumber.

This chapter deals with the main elements; you will find side dishes in the next chapter.

CHRISTMAS DAY TIME PLAN

This might – will – seem irretrievably nerdy, but come Christmas Day, with the present-opening and the kids screaming and all the other distractions, you'll be glad you've made a plan. It will ensure the day goes like a row of dominoes, a row of dominoes that ends in a sumptuous yet stress-free meal.

As I have no idea what menu you'll end up using, I've come up with one of my own. Feel free to borrow. Indeed, nor do I have any idea what time you're eating lunch. Perhaps you're eating dinner. For the purposes of this we'll say the Christmas meal is at 4 p.m. You can adapt and adjust the plan to suit yourself.

This time plan assumes you haven't made anything well in advance to freeze. If you have, defrost in a cool place on Christmas Eve.

MENU

Gravlax on rye crispbreads (p.84)

Classic roast turkey (p.92)
Stuffing (p.136)
Gravy (p.143)
Bread sauce (p.138)
Cranberry sauce (p.139)
Roast potatoes (p.118)
Carrots with harissa, honey
and herbs (p.122)
Sprouts with bacon and hazelnuts (p.126)
Curried leeks with lemon
breadcrumbs (p.132)

Christmas trifle (p.113)

Eccles cakes, cheese (p.114)

UP TO 1 WEEK AHEAD, YOU CAN MAKE:
Gravlax and rye crispbread (p.84)
Cranberry sauce (p.139)

UP TO 3 DAYS AHEAD:
Brine turkey (p.91)
Stuffing (p.136)
Gravy (p.143)
Bread sauce (p.138)
Curried leeks (p.132)
Trifle (p.113)
Eccles cakes (p.114)

CHRISTMAS EVE:

Slice the gravlax, store in the fridge.

Make the herb butter for the turkey and apply.

Parboil the potatoes.

Roast the carrots.

Blanch the sprouts, fry the bacon and onion.

You have now done the lion's share of tomorrow's meal. Bravo.

CHRISTMAS DAY:

7 a.m.	Take the turkey out of the fridge.
10 a.m.	Preheat the oven to 180°C/350°F/Gas mark 4.
10.30 a.m.	In goes the turkey.

Relax, open presents, have a drink, go for a walk, have a snooze.

2 p.m.-ish	Take the turkey out of the oven (depending on size of turkey).
	Turn the oven up to 200°C/400°F/Gas mark 6. Rest the turkey in a warm place.
2.30 p.m.	Roast the potatoes.
3 p.m.	Plate the gravlax.
3.30 p.m.	Final blast for all the bits and pieces:

In the oven, warm up:

Stuffing

Carrots

Leeks

On the hob:

Toss the sprouts in the bacon and onion over a medium–high heat.

Warm the gravy and bread sauce.

4 p.m.	Serve the gravlax.
4.15 p.m.	Carve the turkey, serve with trimmings.

From here I wouldn't want to guess when you'll want pudding, but it's ready when you are. Phew.

REHEATING

As far as possible I've tried to keep the reheating of things in the oven at a consistent temperature. However, should you find that the oven is at a different temperature for, say, roast potatoes or the roast sprouts, then that's fine – just add or knock off a few minutes from the reheating time. Or use the microwave.

SALAD OF CHICORY, ORANGE AND WALNUTS WITH GOAT CURD

SERVES 6–8

500g/1lb 2oz/2 cups goat yogurt

salt and pepper

2–3 heads of chicory, ideally a mix of white and red

1 head of frisée or other lettuce leaves

2–3 oranges

100g/3½oz/¾ cup walnut pieces, roughly chopped

For the dressing

2 tbsp white wine vinegar

2 tsp Dijon mustard

1 tsp sugar

1 garlic clove, lightly squashed

6 tbsp olive oil

a small bunch of parsley, finely chopped

This is a lovely, light – and vegetarian – Christmas Day starter, something to whet the appetite and liven the palate before the onslaught of protein and carbohydrate. If you or yours aren't so fond of goat's milk products then replace the goat yogurt with regular cow's milk yogurt.

2 DAYS AHEAD:
Line a bowl with muslin or a clean tea towel and tip in the yogurt, along with a pinch of salt. Tie up the corners of the towel with string and hang from a cupboard handle or similar, over the bowl. The whey drains out, leaving you with the curd.

UP TO 1 DAY AHEAD (MIN. 1 HOUR);
Make the dressing by putting all the ingredients in a jar along with salt and pepper and shaking furiously until emulsified. Store in a cool place.

Separate the chicory leaves and wash, along with the salad leaves. Dry thoroughly and store, covered in damp kitchen paper, in the fridge. Using a small, sharp knife, slice off the orange peel, taking off all the white pith but taking care not to whip off too much flesh; slice the oranges into thin rounds. Cover and chill. Toast the walnuts in a dry frying pan over a medium heat until fragrant. Set aside.

UP TO 1 HOUR AHEAD:
Arrange the goat curd, chicory, salad leaves, oranges and walnuts on a plate.

TO SERVE:
Spoon the dressing over the salad and serve.

CHEAT: If short of time to make goat curd, beat together 100g/3½oz/scant ½ cup goat yogurt with 200g/7oz soft goat cheese.

GRAVLAX ON RYE CRISPBREAD

SERVES 6–8

a side of salmon, weighing
    around 1kg/2lb 4oz
150g/5½oz/½ cup sea salt
    flakes
75g/2¾oz/⅓ cup light soft
    brown sugar
a bunch of dill,
    finely chopped

For the crispbread

200g/7oz/2 cups rye flour
100g/3½oz/generous ¾ cup
    plain (all-purpose) flour
1 tsp fast-action dried yeast
½ tsp salt
a few twists of pepper
250ml/9fl oz/generous 1 cup
    warm water
2 tsp caraway seeds
    (optional)

To serve

100ml/3½fl oz/7 tbsp sour
    cream
2 tbsp horseradish sauce
2 tbsp capers
1 shallot, very finely chopped
a few sprigs of dill
black pepper
lemon wedges

FREEZABLE (gravlax and
crispbreads)
CHEAT: Use shop-bought
crispbreads. Peter's Yard
are the best.

Gravlax – or gravad lax or gravlaks – is a nifty Scandinavian method of curing fish. It means 'buried salmon', after the medieval method of salting the fish and then burying it in sand. As you do. Though you don't in this recipe. You just bury it in salt and sugar and herbs. It's more delicate than smoked salmon, rather impressive to guests, and yet indescribably easy for you to do.

UP TO 1 WEEK AHEAD (MIN. 48 HOURS):

Line a baking tray with a couple of layers of clingfilm. Lay the salmon on top, skin side down. Mix the salt, sugar and dill, and scatter over the salmon, coating evenly. Cover with clingfilm, then put a board or plate on top, with something heavy to weigh it down. Store in the fridge for 2–3 days, then scrape off excess salt, wrap in clingfilm and return to the fridge.

UP TO 1 WEEK AHEAD (MIN. 4 HOURS):

To make the crispbread, mix the flours, yeast, salt and pepper. Add the warm water and mix to form a dough. On a lightly floured surface, knead for a few minutes. It will be pretty sticky to start, so add a touch more flour if necessary, or use a stand mixer. Put in a bowl and cover with a damp tea towel. Rest for 1 hour.

Preheat the oven to 200°C/400°F/Gas mark 6. Turn the dough out onto a lightly floured surface and roll out to about 3mm/⅛in thick. Scatter over the caraway, if using, and roll a little more. Cut into rounds or rectangles and prick all over with a fork. Transfer to a lightly floured baking sheet and bake for 20–25 minutes until crisp. Cool on a wire rack, then store in an airtight container.

UP TO 1 DAY AHEAD (MIN. 10 MINUTES):

Mix the sour cream and horseradish with a pinch of salt. Cover and chill.

Thinly slice the salmon, taking it off the skin as you slice, then store in the fridge covered with clingfilm.

TO SERVE:

Slather the crispbreads with the horseradish sour cream. Top with slices of gravlax. Scatter over capers, shallot and dill. Add a good twist of black pepper and serve with a wedge of lemon.

SKAGEN PRAWNS

SERVES 4–6

2 egg yolks

1 tsp Dijon mustard

salt and pepper

125ml/4fl oz/½ cup
    grapeseed or groundnut
    (peanut) oil

1 tbsp white wine vinegar

4 tbsp sour cream

2 tbsp finely chopped dill

1 tsp brandy (optional)

500g/1lb 2oz cooked peeled
    prawns (shrimp)

4–6 slices of rye bread or
    sourdough

salmon roe/lumpfish roe
    (optional)

sprigs of dill

lemon wedges

Another Scandi starter. They work so well – fresh and lively and just what you need before the main onslaught. Think of this as a Swedish interpretation of our beloved prawn cocktail.

UP TO 2 DAYS AHEAD (MIN. 30 MINUTES):

In a heavy bowl (or food processor) whisk together the egg yolks and mustard with a pinch of salt. Very slowly add the oil, whisking continuously, until it emulsifies to form a mayonnaise. Add the vinegar, sour cream, dill and brandy, if using. Taste for seasoning and adjust with a little salt or vinegar if necessary. Cover and chill.

UP TO 6 HOURS AHEAD (MIN. 5 MINUTES):

Mix the prawns through the dressing and taste again for seasoning.

TO SERVE:

Toast the bread. Top with the prawns, fish roe and a few dill sprigs. Serve with a wedge of lemon.

CHEAT: Use 150ml/5fl oz/⅔ cup good quality shop-bought mayo instead of making your own.

SCALING UP: If making more mayonnaise, you won't need more egg yolks or brandy.

KIPPER PÂTÉ WITH PICKLED CUCUMBER AND MELBA TOAST

SERVES 6

400g/14oz kipper fillets,
  off the bone
200g/7oz/generous ¾ cup
  unsalted butter, plus extra
  to serve
a pinch of ground mace
a pinch of cayenne pepper
juice of 1 lemon
black pepper
For the melba toast
6 slices of white bread
For the pickled cucumber
150ml/5fl oz/⅔ cup white wine
  vinegar
150g/5½oz/¾ cup caster
  (superfine) sugar
½ tsp fine sea salt
1 shallot, thinly sliced
½ cucumber, thinly sliced
a small bunch of chopped dill

Unashamedly retro is this, and so with any luck something that'll keep both grandparents and young'uns happy. Entirely do-aheadable, too.

UP TO 3 DAYS AHEAD (MIN. 4 HOURS):
Gently poach the kippers in a pan of just-simmering water for 5 minutes, until flaking. Meanwhile, melt the butter in a small pan or microwave. Remove the kippers from the pan and leave to cool for a few minutes. Remove the skin by scraping it away with a knife, discarding any bones and cartilage. Put the kippers in a food processor with three quarters of the melted butter, the mace, cayenne and lemon juice. Add a good twist of pepper and blend until smooth. Spoon into ramekins or a larger serving bowl. Cover with the remaining melted butter, then clingfilm. Chill.

For the melba toast: preheat the oven to 200°C/400°F/ Gas mark 6. Lightly toast the bread in a toaster, remove the crusts, then cut horizontally through the centre of each slice to give you 12 thin slices of toast. Scrape off any excess dough, then cut the pieces into triangles. Bake in the oven for 4–5 minutes until dry and golden. Cool on a wire rack then store in a cool, dry place.

UP TO 6 HOURS AHEAD (MIN. 1 HOUR):
For the pickled cucumber, whisk together the vinegar, sugar and salt until dissolved. Mix with the shallot and cucumber and set aside.

TO SERVE:
Serve the pâté with the melba toast, butter and pickled cucumber.

FREEZABLE (pâté)
CHEAT: Omit the pickle and serve with cornichons (mini pickled gherkins) instead.
SCALING UP: Don't go too strong with the lemon juice – add to taste.

CAULIFLOWER SOUP WITH SPICED CAULIFLOWER FLORETS AND HAZELNUTS

SERVES 6–8

25g/1oz/2 tbsp butter

1 onion, chopped

1 stick of celery, chopped

2 garlic cloves, sliced

a small bunch of thyme

salt and pepper

250g/9oz potatoes, peeled and cubed

1.2 litres/2 pints/5 cups chicken or vegetable stock

700g/1lb 9oz cauliflower florets

2 tbsp walnut oil

½ tsp cumin seeds, roughly crushed

½ tsp coriander seeds, roughly crushed

½ tsp chilli flakes

25g/1oz/¼ cup blanched hazelnuts, roughly chopped

250ml/9fl oz/generous 1 cup double (heavy) cream

A somewhat richer starter for the Christmas binge, one that might be better suited to a fish main course such as the salmon en croute (p.104) than a turkey-with-all-the-trimmings affair. However you could serve it in cute wee espresso cups as a run-up to the main event. Or, sod it, go for broke and gobble a proper bowlful with lots of warm bread and butter before moving onto goose. It's Christmas.

UP TO 3 DAYS AHEAD (MIN. 1 HOUR):

Melt the butter in a large saucepan and add the onion, celery, garlic and thyme. Season with salt and pepper, cover and cook over a low heat for 15 minutes, stirring occasionally, until soft. Remove the thyme.

Add the potatoes and stock, bring to a boil and simmer for 5 minutes, until the potato has started to soften. Add 500g/1lb 2oz of the cauliflower and simmer for 10–15 minutes until tender. Blend until smooth. Taste for seasoning and adjust if necessary. Leave to cool, then cover and chill.

For the spiced cauliflower, break the remaining 200g/7oz into small florets. Heat the oil in a large frying pan over a medium–high heat. Add the spices and stir for 30 seconds, then add the cauliflower. Cook for 4 minutes, stirring and jiggling regularly, until the cauliflower is scorched. Add the hazelnuts and cook for a couple of minutes, then season generously with salt, and tip into a bowl. Leave to cool, then chill.

30 MINUTES AHEAD:

Gently warm through the soup over a low heat, stirring occasionally. Add the cream and keep warm, taking care not to boil. Taste for seasoning and add salt if necessary. Give the cauliflower and hazelnuts another brief encounter in a frying pan to warm through.

TO SERVE:

Ladle the soup into bowls, scatter with the cauliflower and hazelnuts, and serve.

FREEZABLE

RABBIT AND PISTACHIO TERRINE

SERVES 8–10

200g/7oz rindless pork belly,
cubed
1 large rabbit,
or 4 rabbit pieces
250g/9oz chicken livers
50g/1¾oz/4 tbsp unsalted
butter
1 onion, finely chopped
2 garlic cloves, crushed to
a paste
salt and pepper
6 large sage leaves,
finely chopped
a bunch of parsley,
finely chopped
100ml/3½fl oz/7 tbsp Madeira
or medium sherry
100g/3½oz/generous ¾ cup
shelled pistachios
12 rashers of unsmoked
streaky bacon

To serve
bread for toasting
butter
good chutney, preferably
homemade

FREEZABLE
CHEAT: Use 600g/1lb 5oz
skinless, boneless chicken
thighs instead of the rabbit.

While this is an elegant do-ahead Christmas Day starter, it's also rather a handy thing to have sitting quietly in the fridge, ready for you to return late at night, famished and a little refreshed.

Don't be put off by the notion of boning the rabbit – you don't have to do this neatly. If this still seems like too much work, then use 600g/1lb 5oz skinless, boneless chicken thighs.

UP TO 5 DAYS AHEAD (MIN. 1 DAY):

Put the pork belly in a food processor and pulse until coarsely minced. Now take a sharp boning knife and strip the rabbit of all its meat. You need about 600g/1lb 5oz. Put this in the processor along with the chicken livers and any bits of offal that came with the rabbit. Blend to a coarse paste. Scoop out into a bowl.

Preheat the oven to 160°C/325°F/Gas mark 3. Melt the butter in a sauté or frying pan over a gentle heat and add the onion and garlic. Season and cook for 15–20 minutes, stirring occasionally, until soft and golden. Stir through the sage and parsley, then add the Madeira. Whack up the heat and simmer for a few minutes until the liquid has reduced, then add the onion mixture to the meat along with the pistachios, stirring until well combined. Season generously with salt and pepper. Don't skimp on the salt.

Put the bacon rashers under a piece of clingfilm and flatten and stretch out with a rolling pin. Line a 1.5 litre/2½ pint/6 cup loaf tin with a few layers of clingfilm, then line with the bacon, hanging some over the edge. Spoon in the rabbit paste and press lightly, then cover with the excess bacon. Place in a small roasting pan, then add boiling water to come about halfway up the side of the loaf tin. Bake in the oven for 1½ hours.

Remove the terrine from the oven and water bath. Don't tip away the juices in the tin (they are, crucially, reabsorbed). Leave to cool for an hour, then cover in foil. Sit something heavy on top to weigh it down, and chill in the fridge for at least a day.

1 HOUR AHEAD:

Unwrap the terrine and carefully tip it out onto a board.

TO SERVE:

Make some toast. Slice the terrine. Serve with butter and chutney.

THREE WAYS TO COOK YOUR TURKEY

The turkey, the beast, the centrepiece, is surely the greatest headache of all for the Christmas cook. The damn thing is not all that easy to get right. The American chef Grant Achatz put it pretty neatly when he said: 'If you had an oven big enough that you could put a whole cow in, would you expect it all to cook perfectly at the same time?' Of course not. So it's small wonder that something the size of a turkey isn't as easy as you might think to get perfect when cooked in one piece.

Two of the following three recipes, therefore, involve some sort of knifework with your turkey, from simply taking the legs off and cooking them separately, to a slightly more high-tech version. I've kept in a good method for cooking a turkey whole, because I know for many people the presentation of a whole bird is part of the fun of Christmas – and why not? – but for best results I'd get the boning knife out.

BRINING THE TURKEY

The brine
5 litres/9 pints/5 quarts water
300g/10½oz/1 cup fine sea
   salt
This is a salt solution with a ratio of 60g salt:1 litre water. It's up to you which aromatics you add, if any. It'll still have a great effect with just water and salt.

nice aromatics: use some or all
5 bay leaves, roughly chopped
2 bunches of thyme
10 cloves
10 star anise
2 tbsp crushed juniper berries
peel from 1 orange
a bulb of garlic,
   halved horizontally
500ml/18fl oz/generous 2 cups
   porter, stout, or hoppy ale

I also recommend in the strongest possible terms (and I don't do that very often) that you brine the turkey for at least 12 hours to ensure a really tasty, well-seasoned bird. This adds approximately 7 minutes to your personal time in terms of hands-on preparation, and is absolutely worth doing. Again, though, omit if you prefer.

UP TO 3 DAYS AHEAD (MIN. 1 DAY):
Buy a cheap plastic washing-up bowl into which your turkey will fit snugly but not tightly – or use a vast stockpot. Whisk the salt into the water in the bowl, until dissolved, then add any other ingredients you fancy. Lower in the turkey. If there isn't enough liquid to cover the bird, add more water and salt, dissolving before adding it to the bowl and sticking to a ratio of 60g salt per litre of water.

Brine for a minimum of 12 hours and up to 3 days. Rinse the bird, then sit it in a pot of fresh water for an hour or two, changing the water a few times. This prevents over-salting. Pat dry. Now you're ready to cook.

THE CLASSIC TURKEY

SERVES 10–12

200g/7oz/generous ¾ cup
   unsalted butter, softened
2 garlic cloves, crushed to
   a paste
1 tbsp chopped thyme
a big handful of parsley,
   finely chopped
4 sage leaves, finely chopped
1 tbsp rosemary,
   finely chopped
salt and pepper
1 turkey (ideally brined,
   see p.91), about 6kg/13lb,
   wings removed and saved
   for stock (p.171)
a good splash of dry
   white wine

Despite all the arguments in favour of dividing up the turkey and cooking the bits separately, there are still those who will prefer to roast the bird whole, if only for the pleasure of presenting the creature as one. This recipe should ensure that all goes to plan. You'll notice that I don't suggest stuffing the bird – this is in the spirit of evenness of cooking. Cook the stuffing separately (p.136) and then cheat by wanging it up the bird after it's cooked.

Some rules of thumb:

- Take the turkey out of the fridge a good 6 hours before cooking, longer if possible, to bring it up to room temperature.
- Some breeds take longer to cook than others, so use a meat thermometer to keep an eye on the temperature.
- Rest, rest, and rest some more. Minimum 30 minutes, preferably 1 hour, up to 2 hours in a warm place, loosely covered in foil.
- There will almost inevitably be dry bits, I'm afraid. Douse with gravy, or set them to one side and save for one of the leftovers recipes (p.163). Or the dog. Lucky dog.

UP TO 1 DAY AHEAD (MIN. 5 HOURS):

Put the softened butter in a large bowl and beat in the garlic and herbs. Season generously. Now carefully ease your fingers under the skin of the turkey, all around the breast, and then rub the herb butter under the skin. Store in the fridge if necessary.

4–5 HOURS AHEAD:

Preheat the oven to 180°C/350°F/Gas mark 4. Roast the turkey for 20 minutes per kilo plus an extra 90 minutes, basting every hour. There are several variables at play, so during the final 90 minutes keep an eye on the cooking – a skewer into the thickest part of the thigh will come out hot when the bird is cooked. If you have a meat thermometer, the temperature should be 65°C/150°F. Remove from the oven and transfer to a plate or board to rest in a warm place for up to 2 hours, covered loosely in foil.

Tip any excess fat from the roasting pan, then sit the pan over a medium–high heat and add a splash of white wine. Simmer for 5 minutes, scraping up all the sticky bits with a wooden spoon, then tip this into the pre-prepared gravy (p.143).

Carve the turkey and serve when ready.

ROAST TURKEY CROWN WITH CONFIT LEGS

SERVES 10–12

For the crown

1 (ideally brined) turkey,
about 6kg/13lb

150g/5½oz/generous ½ cup
unsalted butter, softened

2 garlic cloves, crushed to
a paste

1 tbsp chopped thyme

a big handful of parsley,
finely chopped

4 large sage leaves,
finely chopped

1 tbsp rosemary,
finely chopped

a good splash of dry
white wine

For the confit legs

2 tbsp salt

700g/1lb 9oz/3 cups duck or
goose fat

2 tbsp brandy

a sprig of thyme

2 sprigs of rosemary

a few pieces of orange peel

black pepper

In which the handsome turkey crown remains intact, and the legs get some juicy French treatment.

UP TO 3 DAYS AHEAD (MIN. 6 HOURS)

Preheat the oven to 150°C/300°F/Gas mark 2. Take the legs off the turkey (YouTube will show you this far more succinctly than I will in words). Remove the wings and save for stock (p.171). Trim off the parson's nose end of the turkey (save also for the stock), so you're left with a neat crown. Put this in the fridge.

Rub the legs all over with the salt. Put the duck fat, brandy, thyme, rosemary and orange peel in a large ovenproof saucepan and melt over a gentle heat. Add the turkey legs and push down to submerge – if they don't fit in one piece then halve between the leg and thigh joint. Season with plenty of pepper, cover, and put in the oven for 3 hours. Remove and leave to cool, then chill. If you need the saucepan then you can transfer the legs to freezer bags, or a large bowl, but keep the fat to help preserve them.

UP TO 1 DAY AHEAD (MIN. 5 HOURS):

Beat together the butter, garlic and herbs, and season with salt and pepper. Carefully loosen the skin of the turkey crown, easing your fingers between skin and flesh, and then rub the herb butter under the skin. Store in the fridge overnight if necessary, though keep in mind that it needs to come out of the fridge a few hours before cooking.

3 HOURS AHEAD:

Preheat the oven to 220°C/425°F/Gas mark 7. Roast the crown for 30 minutes, then turn the oven down to 180°C/350°F/Gas mark 4. Roast for a further 90 minutes, checking your progress after an hour by inserting a skewer into the thickest part of the breast. After 20 seconds, touch it to your lip. If it's hot, the bird's cooked. If not, give it a bit more time. A meat thermometer will give a more accurate reading – it's done at 65°C/150°F. Once the crown is cooked, remove it to a warmed plate or carving board and rest in a warm place, covered loosely in foil. Tip away any excess fat from the roasting pan, then sit the pan over a medium–high heat, add a splash of white wine, and simmer briefly while you scrape up the caramelized bits from the pan using a wooden spoon. Tip this into your pre-prepared gravy (p.143).

90 MINUTES AHEAD;

Warm the confit in the same oven, if there's room, or on a hob over a low heat. After an hour, remove from the goose fat, shred the meat, and rest in a warm place.

TO SERVE:

Carve the breast and serve with the confit leg and trimmings.

SOUS VIDE TURKEY

SERVES 10–12
1 turkey, about 6kg/13lb
a handful of sage leaves
a handful of thyme
a handful of rosemary
150g/5½oz/generous ½ cup
    goose fat or butter, plus
    50g/1¾oz/4 tbsp unsalted
    butter for reheating
2 garlic cloves, finely sliced
salt and pepper

You will also need
food-grade vacuum bags,
    or ziplock bags
a vacuum packer,
    or a hoover
sous vide equipment – either
    a water bath or immersion
    circulator
a large saucepan (at least
    20 litre/4½ gallon/20 quart)
    – only if using an immersion
    circulator

This recipe is both the most cheffy and the most simple of the three turkey recipes in this book. It is cheffy because it uses a cheffy bit of kit, it is simple because, well, once you get going it's entirely stress-free and foolproof. It is also, I believe, the only way there will not be some overcooked turkey breast.

So, *sous vide*. It's French for 'under vacuum', and it involves vacuum packing whatever it is you're cooking, and then putting it in a water bath at a set temperature for a set time. I'm on record as saying that I don't think it's much cop in the home kitchen, but at Christmas the usual rules do not apply. I'm going to cook turkey like this every year. You are guaranteed a really juicy breast, perfectly cooked and tender legs, and – hallelujah! – an oven that is free for other purposes.

NB: with this method there will be a moment where you start questioning my recipe and yourself. You'll think 'there's no way this works' and get in a frightful tizz. Fight this urge. I promise you, promise you, this works.

It's not a cheap bit of kit, the old sous vide, but you can rent one off the internet instead of buying one. There are ways of freestyling with a hob and a thermometer, but at Christmas you probably don't want to keep checking the water temperature.

Omit the brining of the turkey if you prefer/are short of time.

UP TO 4 DAYS AHEAD (MINIMUM 36 HOURS):
Take the breasts, legs and wings off the turkey. If you give plenty of warning your butcher may do it, otherwise have a look on YouTube. Keep the carcass and wings for stock (p.171).

Brine the bird as on p.91, if possible.

UP TO 2 DAYS AHEAD (MIN. 12 HOURS):
If you have brined the turkey, soak it in fresh cold water for an hour or two (as p.91).

If you have a vacuum-packing machine: make sure all the meat is thoroughly dry. Vac-pack the legs with a spoonful of the goose fat or butter, a bunch of herbs and a little sliced garlic. Separately vac-pack the breasts (in individual bags if necessary) with goose fat or butter, herbs and garlic. Store in the fridge.

If you don't have a vac-packer: Put the legs in ziplock bag with a spoonful of the goose fat or butter, a bunch of herbs and a little sliced garlic and lower the (still open) bag into a bowl of water until the legs are just immersed. This should help force out the air. Seal the bags three quarters of the way, then suck out any remaining air with a vacuum cleaner (honestly), and seal completely. Repeat with the breasts.

6 HOURS AHEAD:
Set the water bath to 64°C/147°F. Lower the bags with the legs in and cook for 3 hours. Add the breasts and cook for a further 2 hours.

30–45 MINUTES AHEAD:
Remove the turkey from the water bath and snip out of the bags. Add all the juices to your pre-prepared gravy (p.143), and pat the meat dry with kitchen paper. Heat the butter in a large frying pan and brown the breasts and legs on both sides. Rest in a warm place for up to 30 minutes.

TO SERVE:
Slice and serve with all the trimmings.

FIG AND PROSCIUTTO-STUFFED LOIN OF PORK WITH APPLE SAUCE AND CIDER GRAVY

SERVES 6

a splash of olive oil
100g/3½oz prosciutto,
    finely chopped
1 large onion, finely chopped
salt and pepper
4 fresh figs, roughly chopped
100ml/3½fl oz/7 tbsp Marsala
    wine, or sweet sherry
2 tbsp balsamic vinegar
2kg/4lb 8oz boneless loin
    of pork

For the apple sauce

2 cooking apples,
    peeled, cored and
    roughly chopped
50g/1¾oz/¼ cup caster
    (superfine) sugar
100ml/3½fl oz/7 tbsp water

For the gravy

25g/1oz/2 tbsp butter
2 shallots, sliced
1 garlic clove, finely chopped
1 tbsp plain (all-purpose) flour
200ml/7fl oz/generous ¾ cup
    dry cider
500ml/18fl oz/generous 2 cups
    chicken stock

When it comes to roast pork, it seems the main concern for most people is getting a really good crackling. The best method I've found doesn't involve scoring or salting but, somewhat counter-intuitively, pouring boiling water over the skin before cooking. This makes the skin shrink away from the fat, meaning heat can penetrate the skin better, creating a crisper crackling. Easy.

UP TO 3 DAYS AHEAD (MIN. 4 HOURS):

Heat the oil in a pan over a medium–high heat, and fry the prosciutto until crisp. Add the onion, season with salt and pepper, reduce the heat, cover, and gently sweat for 15–20 minutes until soft. Add the figs, Marsala and vinegar, and simmer uncovered for 15–20 minutes until the figs are collapsing and the sauce is thick. Mash with the back of a spoon until combined and smooth-ish. Taste for seasoning and adjust if necessary, then leave to cool completely. Store in the fridge.

For the apple sauce: put the apples in a pan with the sugar and water. Cover and simmer over a gentle heat for 15 minutes, until the apples are completely soft. Using a wooden spoon, beat to a sauce, cool, cover and chill.

For the gravy: melt the butter over a low heat and add the shallots and garlic. Season with salt and pepper and cook gently for 10–15 minutes until soft. Stir in the flour and cook for a couple of minutes until lightly golden, then add the cider, a splash at a time at first, until well incorporated. Simmer for 5 minutes, then add the stock and simmer for another 20 minutes. Taste for seasoning, then leave to cool. Cover and chill.

UP TO 1 DAY AHEAD (MIN. 3 HOURS):

Make a deep incision in the flesh of the pork loin and stuff with the prosciutto and fig mixture. Tie up with string and chill if doing well ahead.

2 HOURS AHEAD:

Preheat the oven to 220°C/425°F/Gas mark 7. Boil the kettle and pour slowly all over the skin of the pork loin. Rub thoroughly dry, season all over with salt and pepper, and transfer to a

CHEAT: Mix fried prosciutto or bacon through shop-bought fig chutney to make a quick stuffing. You can get decent shop-bought apple sauce, too.

SCALING UP: To bulk up the gravy you can just add more stock, reducing to taste.

roasting pan. Roast for 20 minutes, then turn the oven down to 190°C/375°F/Gas mark 5 and cook for another hour. Remove to a warmed plate and rest in a warm place for 15–30 minutes.

Meanwhile, reheat the gravy, and the apple sauce if you prefer it warm.

TO SERVE:
Carve the pork in fat slices (a bread knife will help to get through the skin) and serve with the gravy and apple sauce.

RARE ROAST SIRLOIN OF BEEF WITH SHALLOTS AND RED WINE

SERVES 6–8

50g/1¾oz/4 tbsp butter

8 banana shallots, halved and peeled

salt and pepper

1 garlic clove, thinly sliced

200ml/7fl oz/generous ¾ cup red wine

400ml/14fl oz/scant 1¾ cups beef stock

a sprig of thyme

1 tbsp redcurrant jelly

1.5kg/3lb 5oz beef sirloin

SCALING: For a smaller or larger piece of beef, add or subtract 1 minute's cooking time for every 100g.

Whatever you sit down to on Christmas Day – turkey, goose, squirrel – there should be at least some sense of occasion. A frisson of the special. I love cottage pie more than most things in life, but I don't want it on Christmas Day. This ticks the 'occasion' box while giving the jaded turkey denier something meaty and fulfilling. It goes nicely with the horseradish sauce on p.142.

Of course, with rare beef the scope for doing ahead is diminished, though not nixed entirely. A blast in a super-hot oven followed by a long rest wrapped in lots of foil will give you plenty of time and oven space to cook the other bits and pieces.

UP TO 1 DAY AHEAD (MIN. 2 HOURS):

Melt the butter in a saucepan over a medium heat and add the shallots. Season with salt and pepper and cook for a few minutes until they start to colour, then add the garlic and wine. Simmer over a medium–high heat for 5–7 minutes, then add the stock and the thyme. Bring back to a boil, then cook over a medium–low heat for about an hour, until reduced and sticky. Stir in the redcurrant jelly, taste for seasoning, and set aside. Cool and chill if necessary.

4 HOURS AHEAD:

Take the beef out of the fridge.

2 HOURS AHEAD:

Preheat the oven to 220°C/425°F/Gas mark 7.

Season the beef generously. Get a large frying pan hot over a high heat and brown the beef all over. Transfer to a roasting pan and roast in the oven for 20 minutes. Remove and wrap tightly in several layers of foil. Rest in a warm place for an hour. (And you've got a hot oven ready for your roast potatoes.)

30 MINUTES AHEAD:

Put the red wine gravy over a gentle heat and warm through.

TO SERVE:

Just before carving tip the meat juices from the foil into the gravy. Carve in thin slices and serve with the shallot gravy.

ROAST GOOSE WITH POTATO, APPLE AND CHESTNUT STUFFING

SERVES 6–8
5–6kg/11–13lb goose
1 onion, finely chopped
25g/1oz/2 tbsp butter
salt and pepper
7 large sage leaves,
   finely chopped
a big bunch of parsley,
   finely chopped
1 tbsp chopped thyme
100g/3½oz cooked chestnuts,
   finely chopped
2 cooking apples, peeled,
   cored and roughly
   chopped
juice of ½ orange
2 large potatoes, peeled
   and cubed
4 slices of brown bread,
   toasted and finely
   chopped into
   breadcrumbs

It is almost impossible to write about goose without mentioning Dickens. Roast goose is the centrepiece of the Cratchits' festive dinner in *A Christmas Carol*, and is so splendid a specimen that 'Bob said he didn't believe there ever was such a goose cooked', while Tiny Tim bangs the table with his knife and cries 'Hurrah!' I hope this recipe brings you as much joy.

UP TO 2 DAYS AHEAD (MIN. 6 HOURS):
Untruss the goose if necessary, and remove giblets (saving these for the gravy p.143) and excess fat (for roast potatoes p.118).

In a large pan, gently fry the onion in the butter with some salt and pepper until soft. Add sage, parsley, thyme, chestnuts, apples and orange juice to the onion along with a small splash of water. Cover and simmer gently until the apples are collapsing.

Meanwhile, boil the potatoes in salted water until tender, then drain. Add the potatoes to the apple mixture and mash thoroughly, then add the breadcrumbs. Beat together, taste for seasoning and adjust if necessary. Leave to cool completely, then stuff the goose with the cold stuffing. Cover and chill.

6 HOURS AHEAD:
Remove the goose from the fridge.

4 HOURS AHEAD:
Preheat the oven to 190°C/375°F/Gas mark 5. Rub the bird all over with salt and pepper. Roast for 2½–3 hours. Every 30 minutes, remove from the oven and baste with the fat collected in the pan. Pour off excess fat through a sieve and save for roast potatoes.

Remove the goose from the oven and rest in a warm place for at least 30 minutes, ideally an hour, loosely covered in foil.

UP TO 30 MINUTES AHEAD:
Remove the legs and strip off the meat, which should come away easily. Cover with foil and keep warm.

TO SERVE:
I find it easiest to take the breasts off whole, and then carve into slices. Serve a couple of slices of breast and some leg meat with a good spoonful of stuffing and sides of your choice.

FREEZABLE: You can make the stuffing ahead and freeze it. Defrost a day before using.

SALMON EN CROUTE WITH HOLLANDAISE SAUCE

SERVES 6–8

25g/1oz/2 tbsp butter

4 shallots, chopped

1 garlic clove, finely chopped

salt and pepper

2 tbsp pine nuts

200g/7oz kale or cavolo nero, hard stalks discarded, then roughly chopped

6 anchovy fillets

zest and juice of 1 lemon

2 x roughly equal pieces of salmon fillet, about 500–600g/1lb 2oz–1lb 5oz each, skinned

500g/1lb 2oz puff pastry (preferably 'all butter')

1 egg, beaten

For the hollandaise

2 egg yolks

250g/9oz/generous 1 cup unsalted butter

juice of 1 lemon

a pinch of cayenne pepper

To serve

fresh watercress

dill

salmon caviar

If you're planning on serving fish on Christmas Day then you need something suitably significant and festive, decorous and decorative. Ideally you also want something you can prep well in advance and then just pop in the oven when the time comes. Which is what this does.

Hollandaise is generally done in a last-minute panic, as it doesn't tend to do well from sitting around for too long – but you can sidestep this up to a point by doing it an hour or so ahead and storing in a thermos flask.

By all means omit the garnish but, being Christmas, a bell here and a whistle there is perhaps expected.

UP TO 3 DAYS AHEAD (MIN. 4 HOURS):

Melt the butter in a large pan and add the shallots and garlic. Season with salt and pepper, cover and cook over a gentle heat for 15 minutes, until soft. Meanwhile, toast the pine nuts in a dry frying pan for a few minutes, until golden. Add the kale, anchovies, lemon zest and juice and pine nuts to the shallots. Cover and cook for 5–10 minutes, until the kale has wilted, then tip into a food processor and blend to a rough paste. Taste for seasoning and adjust if necessary. Leave to cool completely, then store in the fridge.

UP TO 1 DAY AHEAD (MIN. 2 HOURS):

Trim the salmon and remove any bones with a pair of tweezers. Lay one piece on a board, with the skinned side facing down. Spread with the stuffing as evenly as possible, and then top with the other piece of salmon, skinned side up.

On a lightly floured surface roll out the pastry to a rectangle roughly 45 x 30cm/18 x 12in, and 3mm/$\frac{1}{8}$in thick. Brush the edges with beaten egg, then lay the salmon down the middle. Fold the pastry up over the salmon and pinch to seal the edges all around, then turn over so the join is underneath and place on a lightly floured baking sheet. Cover in clingfilm and chill.

[method continues on p.106]

1 HOUR AHEAD:

Preheat the oven to 190°C/375°F/Gas mark 5.

Using the blunt side of a knife, mark a criss-cross pattern on the pastry. Brush all over with beaten egg, then bake for 40–45 minutes, until golden.

Meanwhile, make the hollandaise: melt the butter in a small pan. Bring 3cm/1¼in of water to a boil in a separate saucepan, then reduce the heat to just below a simmer. Put the egg yolks in a heavy heatproof bowl and sit over the pan of barely-simmering water. Whisk for a minute or so, until the yolks start to streak the sides of the bowl. Slowly add the melted butter in a gentle, steady stream, whisking all the time, until fully incorporated and thickened. Should the sauce split, start again with 2 fresh egg yolks over the simmering water, and slowly add the curdled first batch to these yolks, then continue. Take off the heat and whisk in the lemon juice, cayenne, and a pinch of salt. Keep warm in a thermos flask if necessary.

When the pastry is golden and crisp, remove from the oven and carefully transfer to a serving board to rest for 5–10 minutes. Garnish with fresh watercress, blobs of caviar and dill sprigs.

TO SERVE:

Cut the salmon into fat slices. Serve with the hollandaise sauce.

CHEAT: Skip making the stuffing if short of time, and use a good-quality shop-bought pesto.

JERUSALEM ARTICHOKE AND GRUYÈRE PIE

SERVES 6

55g/2oz/4 tbsp unsalted butter

1 large onion, thinly sliced

2 garlic cloves, finely chopped

salt and pepper

300g/10½oz Jerusalem artichokes

125g/4½oz new potatoes, peeled and quartered

125g/4½oz cauliflower florets

15g/½oz/2 tbsp plain (all-purpose) flour

250ml/9fl oz/generous 1 cup whole milk, warmed

40g/1½oz Gruyère cheese, grated

1 tbsp Dijon mustard

a good grating of nutmeg

500g/1lb 2oz puff pastry

1 egg, beaten

This is based on a recipe by the great chef Yotam Ottolenghi, whose version differs, among other ways, in its use of anchovies. By all means add these to the mix, though as this is intended as a vegetarian dish, I've left them out.

UP TO 3 DAYS AHEAD (MIN. 2 HOURS):

Melt 40g/1½oz/3 tbsp of the butter in a large pan and add the onion and garlic. Season with salt and pepper and cook over a low heat for 20 minutes, stirring occasionally, until soft and golden.

Meanwhile, scrub the Jerusalem artichokes, then peel and cut into walnut-sized pieces. Put in a large pan of salted water with the potatoes. Bring to a boil and simmer for 5 minutes. Add the cauliflower and simmer for 5–7 minutes, until the vegetables are tender, then drain. Leave to steam until dry. Set aside.

Melt the remaining butter in a pan. Add the flour and stir for a minute until combined and starting to colour, then slowly add the warm milk, stirring continuously until thick and glossy. Take off the heat and add the cheese, mustard and nutmeg. Season to taste, mix with the vegetables and onions, and leave to cool.

Divide the pastry in two. Line a baking tray with lightly floured baking parchment. Flour a work surface and roll each sheet of pastry out to about 3mm/⅛in thick. Cut out two large rounds, one a couple of inches larger than the other. Put the smaller round on the tray. Brush the edge with beaten egg, then put the filling in the middle, leaving a 2.5cm/1in border around the edge. Lay the large pastry round on top and seal the rim, pressing with a fork. Cut a little opening in the top of the pastry (to let air out), then with a blunt knife draw a pretty series of semicircles around the pastry. Chill for 30 minutes, or longer.

Preheat the oven to 200°C/400°F/Gas mark 6. Brush the pastry with beaten egg, then bake for 40 minutes until golden and crisp. Serve, or leave to cool, cover and chill.

45 MINUTES AHEAD:

Preheat the oven to 200°C/400°F/Gas mark 6. Reheat the pie for 20–25 minutes until hot in the middle (check using a skewer).

TO SERVE:

Slice the pie and serve.

FREEZABLE

NUT ROAST

SERVES 6–8
25g/1oz/2 tbsp butter
1 onion, finely chopped
1 garlic clove, finely chopped
1 stick of celery,
    finely chopped
5–6 outer leaves of
    a savoy cabbage
500g/1lb 2oz parsnips, peeled
    and cut into chunks
4 portobello or field
    mushrooms, sliced
100g/3½oz/¾ cup hazelnuts,
    chopped
100g/3½oz/¾ cup almonds,
    chopped
a generous handful of
    chopped herbs,
    such as parsley, thyme,
    tarragon, chives
2 slices of brown bread,
    toasted and chopped
    or torn
2 eggs
olive oil
salt and pepper

Nut roast. Two words that have the ability to fill most of us with not a small amount of trepidation. For me this is largely down to its association with the slightly anaemic-looking vegetarian kid at school, who'd be left to poke a grey and claggy sponge of a lunch around his plate while the rest of us piled into roast beef.

And yet, there's absolutely nothing to say this shouldn't be a delicious and hearty alternative to a roast or, why not, something to sit merrily alongside one.

UP TO 3 DAYS AHEAD (MIN. 3 HOURS):
Melt the butter in a large pan and gently sweat the onion, garlic and celery until soft. Meanwhile, bring a pan of salted water to a boil. Add the cabbage leaves and cook for 30 seconds, then remove with tongs and plunge into a bowl of cold water. Leave until cool, then drain and dry. Boil the parsnips in the same water until tender, then drain.

Add the mushrooms to the onion mixture and gently cook until softened, then add the parsnips, nuts and herbs. Transfer all this to a food processor along with the toast and eggs, and pulse until combined but not too smooth. Taste for seasoning and adjust if necessary. Leave to cool completely.

Lightly grease a 1.5 litre/2½ pint/6 cup loaf tin with oil or butter. Cut out the tougher ribs from the centre of the cabbage leaves, then line the tin with the leaves. Fill with the nut filling, and top with last of the cabbage leaves. Wrap tightly in clingfilm and chill.

1 HOUR AHEAD:
Preheat the oven to 180°C/350°F/Gas mark 4. Brush the top cabbage leaves with olive oil and season with salt. Bake for 45 minutes. The cabbage may start to catch – I like this, but if you don't, cover loosely with foil. Keep warm until ready to serve.

TO SERVE:
Tip onto a board, slice, and serve.

FREEZABLE

FIGGY PUDDING WITH BRANDY BUTTER

SERVES 6–8 (WITH PROBABLY
NOT INCONSIDERABLE
LEFTOVERS)

250g/9oz dried figs

100g/3½oz/7 tbsp unsalted
butter, softened

100ml/3½fl oz/7 tbsp brandy,
plus extra to finish

250g/9oz/1½ cups mixed
sultanas, raisins
and currants

250g/9oz apples, peeled,
cored and very finely
chopped or grated

125g/4½oz/generous ½ cup
dark soft brown sugar

75g/2¾oz/¾ cup dried
breadcrumbs

75g/2¾oz/generous ½ cup
self-raising flour

2 tsp ground allspice

½ tsp salt

For the candied peel

1 large orange

200g/7oz/1 cup caster
(superfine) sugar

200ml/7fl oz/generous ¾ cup
water

For the brandy butter

200g/7oz/generous ¾ cup
cool (not cold) unsalted
butter, diced

200g/7oz/1 cup soft light
brown sugar

zest of ½ lemon

3 tbsp brandy

50g/1¾oz/½ cup ground
almonds (if necessary)

Figgy pudding is Christmas pudding's ever-so-slightly paler and fig-spiked sister. I particularly like what the figs bring to the party, both texturally and in terms of flavour. Traditionally the ingredients are mixed on the last Sunday of November (Stir-Up Sunday) and left to commune for a while before cooking, but I say why not crack on and bake the thing then, too. Three and a bit weeks' head start will ensure you have a deliciously rich and juicy pudding come Christmas day. The homemade candied peel might seem a faff but it's straightforward enough, and makes all the difference.

UP TO 3 MONTHS AHEAD (MIN. 2 WEEKS):

To make the candied peel, using a small sharp knife, score the orange peel in quarters without cutting into the flesh, then take it off the orange. Cut into thin strips, then boil in a pan of water for 10 minutes; drain and repeat. This gets rid of the bitterness. Put the sugar and water in a pan and bring to a boil, stirring to dissolve the sugar. Add the peel and simmer gently for 1 hour, swirling the pan every now and then, and turning down the heat if it starts to colour. When the liquid is thick and sticky, use tongs to transfer the peel to a wire rack and leave until completely cool and dry. Chop most of it finely, saving a little for the garnish if you like. Don't throw away the cooking syrup.

Finely chop about 100g/3½oz of the figs. Put the rest in a food processor with the butter and the brandy. Blend until smooth, then scoop into a mixing bowl. Add the chopped figs, finely chopped orange peel, the dried fruit, apples, sugar, breadcrumbs, flour, allspice, salt, and the reserved orange syrup. Stir enthusiastically.

Grease a 1.5 litre/2½ pint/6 cup pudding bowl with butter (first making sure it will fit inside a large saucepan), then line its base with a circle of baking parchment. Scoop in the pudding mix. Top with a piece of buttered baking parchment, then cover tightly with a couple of layers of foil. Scrunch up another piece of foil and put it in the bottom of a large saucepan and sit the bowl on top of this (you don't want it touching the bottom).

[method continues on p.112]

FIGGY PUDDING [CONTINUED FROM P.110]

Boil the kettle and add boiling water to come halfway up the side of the pudding bowl. Cover the pan and simmer over a gentle heat for about 3 hours, topping up with boiling water when necessary. Remove and store in a cool, dry place.

UP TO 3 DAYS AHEAD (MIN. 30 MINUTES):

To make the brandy butter, beat together the butter and sugar until creamed. Beat in the lemon zest, and then slowly beat in the brandy. If it looks as though it's thinking about curdling, a small handful of ground almonds will set it right. Cover and store in the fridge.

2 HOURS AHEAD:

Repeat the foil-in-saucepan procedure. Gently simmer the pudding for an hour or two. Carefully turn onto a serving plate. Garnish with the reserved candied peel and a sprig of holly if you like.

Alternatively, you can reheat the pudding in a microwave. Give it 15–20 minutes on medium.

TO SERVE:

Heat some brandy on the hob, making sure you don't let it boil. Tip the brandy over the pudding and set it alight. Dish up the Christmas pudding with the brandy butter. Have a lie down.

FREEZABLE

CHEAT: Instead of making candied peel, use 200g/7oz chopped mixed peel.

CHRISTMAS TRIFLE

SERVES 8–10

For the jelly

3 gelatine leaves, or 1 sachet powdered gelatine

150g/5½oz/¾ cup caster (superfine) sugar

250ml/9fl oz/generous 1 cup water

100ml/3½fl oz/7 tbsp kirsch or cassis

200g/7oz maraschino or glacé (candied) cherries

In the bottom

200g/7oz savoiardi biscuits or trifle sponge

100ml/3½fl oz/7 tbsp medium sherry

For the plums

100g/3½oz/½ cup caster (superfine) sugar

400g/14oz plums, stoned and quartered

1 cinnamon stick

2 star anise

For the custard

400ml/14 fl oz/scant 1¾ cups double (heavy) cream

1 vanilla pod, split down the middle

4 egg yolks

75g/2¾oz/⅓ cup caster (superfine) sugar

To finish

400ml/14 fl oz/scant 1¾ cups double (heavy) cream

toasted flaked (slivered) almonds

pomegranate seeds

Trifle – a dessert that is every bit as momentous as the traditional figgy pudding, and one that will for many be more welcome. I've gone big here – spiced plums, booze-soaked cherries, kirsch, sherry. It's Christmas, after all. Just don't set it on fire.

UP TO 3 DAYS AHEAD (MIN. 8 HOURS):

Soak the gelatine leaves, if using, in cold water for 10 minutes, then squeeze out the excess water. Put the gelatine in a pan with the sugar, water and kirsch. Warm over a gentle heat, swirling the pan occasionally, until the sugar and gelatine have dissolved completely. Add the cherries and take off the heat.

In your most handsome – ideally glass – bowl (or individual glasses), create a layer of biscuits or sponge and spritz over the sherry. Pour the cherry jelly over, then chill for 3–4 hours until set.

Meanwhile, put the sugar, plums, cinnamon and star anise in a pan with a splash of water. Cover and cook over a medium heat for 15 minutes until the plums have collapsed. Discard the spices and set aside (refrigerate if making this well ahead).

For the custard, put the cream and vanilla in a pan over a low heat and slowly bring to a boil. In a heavy, heatproof bowl, whisk together the egg yolks and sugar until pale and fluffy. When the cream is at a rolling boil, dump it straight onto the egg mixture, whisking furiously, and continue to whisk for 20 seconds. Leave it for 2 minutes. It should now thickly coat the back of a wooden spoon. If not, sit the bowl over a pan of gently simmering water and stir constantly until it does. Leave to cool completely.

Pour the custard over the set jelly and return to the fridge for a couple of hours, until the custard has set.

UP TO 6 HOURS AHEAD (MIN. 30 MINUTES):

Top the custard with the plums. Whip the cream until soft peaks form, then spoon over the plums, and decorate with the almonds and pomegranate seeds. Cover and chill until ready to serve.

TO SERVE:

Spoon into bowls, making sure everyone gets a bit of each layer.

CHEAT: Use a good quality shop-bought custard.

ECCLES CAKES (FOR CHEESE)

MAKES 8–10 CAKES

500g/1lb 2oz puff pastry

2 egg whites, lightly beaten

demerara sugar

For the filling

40g/1½oz/3 tbsp unsalted
   butter

225g/8oz/1½ cups currants

75g/2¾oz/⅓ cup light
   muscovado sugar

zest of ½ lemon

1 tsp mixed spice

a pinch of salt

If you're omitting the Christmas pud in favour of cheese then these tick both boxes, in that they contain currants, and are sensational with a piece of Stilton or Cheddar. This recipe owes a great debt to Fergus Henderson, at whose restaurant, St. John, I first encountered the joys of Eccles cake with tangy cheese.

If you want to make your own puff pastry then good for you, but you'll have to find the recipe elsewhere.

UP TO 3 DAYS AHEAD:

For the filling, melt the butter in a pan and mix through the other ingredients. Leave to cool.

Roll out the pastry to about 3mm/⅛ in thick and use an 8cm/3¼in cutter to cut out 8–10 rounds. Put a good spoonful of the filling in the centre and brush the edges of the pastry with egg white. Fold the edges up into the centre and pinch to seal, then flip over, shape into a round, and place on a lightly floured baking sheet. Lightly roll over the cakes to flatten a little. Slash the pastry a couple of times on top with a sharp knife, brush with egg white, dust with demerara sugar, and chill for 30 minutes.

Meanwhile, preheat the oven to 220°C/425°F/Gas mark 7. Bake for 15–20 minutes, until golden and sticky. Cool on a wire rack and store in an airtight container, or freeze until needed.

FREEZABLE

SCALING UP: You shouldn't need more egg whites.

SIDES

The Christmas binge is as much about the side dishes as it is about the centrepiece. Particularly for those who aren't crazy about turkey, it's crucial that the roast potatoes, the gravy, and all the other satellites are on the money. And while these bits and pieces can involve a certain amount of preparation, most of that preparation can be done a day, sometimes even a week, in advance.

It took too many Christmases for me to clock onto the fact that you didn't have to make bread sauce on Christmas morn, that sprouts and spuds could be parboiled on Christmas Eve, and that gravy not only *could* be done ahead, but actually benefited from it.

This is the perfect time to rope in family and those guests who disingenuously offer a hand while backing towards the door. 'Well yes, actually,' you can say, while thrusting a potato peeler in their direction. With jobs of peeling, trimming, chopping and slicing delegated, you can focus on things like having a bath.

ROAST POTATOES

SERVES 6–8

1.5kg/3lb 5oz floury potatoes,
   such as King Edward or
   Maris Piper
100g/3½oz/7 tbsp beef
   dripping
sea salt and freshly ground
   black pepper

Making a successful roast potato is far simpler than you think. There are a few important rules to follow, but follow them and you will end up with some world-beating spuds. Namely:

- Parboiling shouldn't involve boiling the potatoes for a minute or two. They should be almost cooked when they meet the oven. This means you don't have to muck about shaking them to fluff up the edges.
- Parboiling well in advance will mean the potatoes are good and dry, giving a better, crisper crust.
- A crowded oven won't help – the hot air needs to get around the potatoes and crisp them up. I realize that at Christmas this isn't necessarily straightforward but there it is.
- Resist turning them every 10 minutes. Just leave them. And leave them some more.
- Salt.
- Follow these rules and it doesn't particularly matter what fat you use, though for flavour I prefer beef dripping.

1 DAY AHEAD (MIN. 2 HOURS):

Peel the potatoes and cut into the size you like the most. Put in a pan of fresh water with a good pinch of salt. Bring to a boil and simmer for 8–12 minutes (depending on size) until they're just about cooked but not quite. Gently drain in a colander. Leave for a few minutes to steam dry, then tip onto a baking tray. When cool and dry, cover and chill, or freeze. Should they discolour, don't fret – this won't affect flavour or texture, or indeed colour, once roasted.

90 MINUTES AHEAD:

Preheat the oven to 200°C/400°F/Gas mark 6 (if it's already in use at, say 220°C/425°F/Gas mark 7, that's fine).

Put a sturdy roasting pan over a medium–high heat and add the dripping. Let it fizzle and melt. When it has gone silent, carefully add the potatoes, taking care not to splash the hot fat about the place. Season with a hefty wallop of sea salt and black pepper, and prod around the tray until the spuds are all coated in the dripping. Transfer to the oven and roast for an hour or so, giving a shake and a turn after about 45 minutes.

Done, as Gordon Ramsay would say.

A FEW TWISTS

- Add 2 quartered lemons, a few rosemary sprigs, and the unpeeled cloves from a bulb of garlic to the potatoes before roasting.
- Mix 100g/3½oz/scant 1 cup grated Parmesan with 50g/1¾oz/scant ½ cup semolina flour and toss through the potatoes before roasting.
- For a smoky, spicy twist, add 1 tbsp hot smoked paprika before roasting.
- Get hold of some truffle salt and season the potatoes with this just before serving.

SHREDDED RAW VEGETABLE SALAD

SERVES 6–8

3 tbsp pine nuts

200g/7oz carrots, peeled

200g/7oz beetroot, peeled
(wearing rubber gloves,
if preferred)

200g/7oz cauliflower

100g/3½oz radishes, washed

100g/3½oz kale, stripped off
its stalks and washed

a handful of pomegranate
seeds

a handful of mint leaves,
shredded

a handful of parsley,
roughly chopped

For the dressing

juice of 1 lemon

6 tbsp olive oil

1 banana shallot, thinly sliced

1 tsp crushed coriander seeds

½ tsp crushed cumin seeds

½ tsp sugar

salt and pepper

Amid the delicious barrage of fat and protein that is the Christmas meal, something fresh, crunchy and lively such as this is quite welcome. You can muck around with which vegetables you use based, perhaps, on what other sides you're serving. This combination works well though. Eat after you've gobbled everything else. Amazingly you'll find you suddenly have room for Christmas pudding. Or more turkey.

UP TO 3 DAYS AHEAD (MIN. 5 MINUTES):

Make the dressing by shaking all the ingredients together in a jar, or whisking in a small bowl. Store in the fridge.

In a dry frying pan over a medium heat, toast the pine nuts until golden and fragrant, taking care not to burn. Cool, then store in a jar or small bowl.

UP TO 6 HOURS AHEAD (MIN. 30 MINUTES):

Grate the carrots and beetroot (wearing gloves if you don't want pink hands for the day). Thinly slice the cauliflower and radishes. Roughly chop the kale. Mix this all together and set aside.

UP TO 1 HOUR AHEAD:

Toss the shredded vegetables with the pine nuts, pomegranate seeds and herbs, then mix through the dressing. It's ready to serve when you are.

CARROTS WITH HARISSA, HONEY AND HERBS

SERVES 6–8
750g/1lb 10oz small–medium
   sized carrots, scrubbed
a bulb of garlic, cloves
   separated but unpeeled
3 tbsp olive oil
a few sprigs of thyme
   and rosemary
1 tbsp harissa
2 tbsp runny honey
salt and pepper
20g/¾oz herbs, such as
   parsley, tarragon, mint,
   chervil, chives

Unless working with enormo-carrots, I find roasting them whole preferable on most levels: easier to prep, prettier to serve, and seemingly more flavourful. (If you do find yourself with enormo-carrots, halve or quarter them vertically.)

Harissa is a Middle Eastern spice paste and is available in the supermarket.

UP TO 1 DAY AHEAD (MIN. 2 HOURS):
Preheat the oven to 200°C/400°F/Gas mark 6, or thereabouts. Toss the carrots and garlic in the oil, thyme, rosemary, harissa and honey, and season with salt and pepper. Roast for 40–45 minutes, until tender but with still a bit of bite. Cool, cover, and chill.

30 MINUTES AHEAD:
Warm the carrots through in an oven at around 200°C/400°F/Gas mark 6. Roughly chop the remaining herbs.

TO SERVE:
Toss the herbs through the warm carrots with another glug of olive oil, and serve.

SCALING UP: Go easy on the garlic, oil, harissa and honey.

KALE WITH PINE NUTS AND LEMON ZEST

SERVES 6–8

500g/1lb 2oz kale, cavolo
    nero or savoy cabbage,
    tough stalks discarded,
    leaves shredded
2 tbsp pine nuts or flaked
    (slivered) almonds
2 tbsp olive oil
salt and pepper
zest of 1 lemon

There's the enduring perception that green vegetables ought to be done last minute, and in a matter of seconds, to prevent ruination. This isn't strictly true. They can all, I think without exception, be part-cooked in advance and plunged into iced water – blanching. This means that when you finish them off at the last minute it takes a fraction of the time, and there is less scope for overcooking or sogginess.

UP TO 1 DAY AHEAD:

Fill a big bowl with cold water and add a few ice cubes. Bring a large pan of salted water to a boil and add the kale. Simmer for 30 seconds, then drain, run briefly under a cold tap, and dump into the cold water. Leave for a few minutes until cold, then drain and squeeze out the excess water. Cover and chill.

In a dry frying pan over a medium heat, toast the pine nuts until golden and fragrant. Cool, then store in a jar or small bowl.

10 MINUTES AHEAD:

Heat the oil in a large saucepan over a medium–high heat and add the kale. Season with salt and pepper and stir for a couple of minutes until heated through. Add the pine nuts and lemon zest and serve.

SCALING UP: Blanch the kale in batches if necessary. You won't need any more oil for reheating greater quantities.

BRUSSELS SPROUTS

To say you don't like sprouts is, I would argue, like saying you don't like music. Perhaps you don't like them done a certain way, just like you won't like certain music, but they're such versatile wee things that there's surely *bound* to be some iteration of these miniature cabbages that blows your hair back. I've given you three options below, one of which, granted, isn't strictly 'do-ahead', but is too good to omit.

BRUSSELS SPROUT PURÉE WITH CREAM AND NUTMEG

SERVES 6–8

500g/1lb 2oz sprouts, trimmed and halved
25g/1oz/2 tbsp butter, softened
100ml/3½fl oz/7 tbsp double (heavy) cream
a good grating of nutmeg
a squeeze of lemon juice
salt and pepper

UP TO 1 DAY AHEAD:
Bring a pan of salted water to a boil and add the sprouts. Simmer for 7–8 minutes until completely tender. Drain thoroughly, then blend in a food processor with the butter, cream, nutmeg, a squeeze of lemon and a pinch of salt and pepper. Transfer to an ovenproof serving dish and leave to cool, then cover and chill.

45 MINUTES AHEAD:
Preheat the oven to 200°C/400°F/Gas mark 6. Cover the purée with foil and warm in the oven for 20–25 minutes, stirring halfway through. Keep warm until ready to serve. You could do all this in a microwave (using clingfilm instead of foil).

ROAST SPROUTS

SERVES 6–8

750g/1lb 10oz sprouts, trimmed
2 tbsp olive oil
salt and pepper

The notion of roasting greens is slightly alien to us but it's something I'm doing more and more. I adore the slightly burnt flavour, the way the outer leaves char at the edges.

This isn't the most do-ahead of dishes, but as they only need a 10-minute blast before serving everything else, they will keep warm quite happily.

20 MINUTES AHEAD:
Preheat the oven to as hot as it can go. Toss the sprouts in olive oil, salt and pepper, then roast for 7–10 minutes until charred and tender. Serve.

SPROUTS WITH BACON AND HAZELNUTS

SERVES 6–8

500g/1lb 2oz sprouts, trimmed
and washed
2 rashers of smoked streaky
bacon, finely chopped
1 tsp vegetable oil
25g/1oz/2 tbsp unsalted
butter
1 small onion, finely chopped
20g/¾oz/3 tbsp blanched
hazelnuts, roughly
chopped
salt and pepper

UP TO 1 DAY AHEAD (MIN. 30 MINUTES):

Bring a pan of salted water to a boil and add the sprouts. Simmer for 4–5 minutes, drain, then plunge into a bowl of iced water. Leave until cool, then drain again and shake dry.

In a large frying pan, fry the bacon in the oil until crisp. Remove to a small bowl. In the same pan, add the butter and gently fry the onion until soft and golden, then add the hazelnuts, salt and pepper, and fry for a couple more minutes until the hazelnuts start to turn golden. Tip all of this into the bowl with the bacon. Cool, cover, and chill.

15 MINUTES AHEAD:

Put the bacon, onion and hazelnuts back into a large frying pan over a medium–high heat. Once sizzling, add the sprouts and stir-fry for 4–5 minutes until heated through. Transfer to a serving dish and keep warm until ready to serve.

BEETROOT AND ANCHOVY GRATIN

SERVES 6–8

300ml/10fl oz/1¼ cups double (heavy) cream
1 garlic clove, squished with the flat of a knife
a sprig of thyme
2 tbsp horseradish sauce
salt and pepper
650–700g/about 1lb 8oz beetroot, washed
a little softened butter
12 anchovy fillets

One of my all-time favourite side dishes, and one that enthrones beetroot in my mind as the king of vegetables. Here, that noble root is bathed in cream, garlic, thyme and anchovy. Incredibly simple, outrageously good. It's particularly effective with beef or pork, though I shouldn't have thought there'll be too many complaints if you serve it with the turkey.

UP TO 3 DAYS AHEAD (MIN. 90 MINUTES):

Put the cream, garlic, thyme and horseradish in a small pan with a good pinch of salt and pepper. Gently warm until it's thinking about boiling. Take off the heat and leave to infuse for 30 minutes. Meanwhile, preheat the oven to 190°C/375°F/Gas mark 5.

Peel and slice the beetroot (wearing rubber gloves to avoid pink hands). Rub an ovenproof dish with softened butter, then layer up the beetroot and anchovy. Strain the cream through a sieve over the beetroot. Bake for 45 minutes. If not serving immediately, leave to cool, cover and chill.

45 MINUTES AHEAD:

Preheat the oven to 200°C/400°F/Gas mark 6. Reheat the beetroot for 20–25 minutes. Keep warm until ready to serve.

FREEZABLE

SCALING UP: Extra garlic won't be necessary if making this in larger quantities.

BRAISED FENNEL WITH ORANGE AND VERMOUTH

SERVES 6–8
3 fennel bulbs
50g/1¾oz/4 tbsp butter
salt and pepper
100ml/3½fl oz/7 tbsp dry
    vermouth
zest and juice of 1 orange

This goes particularly well with the salmon en croute (p.104), though would be quite content alongside any main dish, providing a sweet, aniseed foil to something more robust.

UP TO 1 DAY AHEAD (MIN. 30 MINUTES):

Trim the fennel, reserving the fronds. Quarter them through the root. In a large sauté or saucepan, melt the butter over a medium heat until frothing. Add the fennel and season with salt and pepper. Cook for about 10 minutes, turning occasionally, until nicely coloured. Add the vermouth and orange, and simmer for 5 minutes. Cover and cook for a further 5 minutes until soft, then take off the heat. If not serving immediately, leave to cool, then cover and chill.

15 MINUTES AHEAD:

Reheat the fennel in a hot oven or over a medium heat. Garnish with the fennel fronds, and serve.

SCALING UP: If making a larger batch go easy on the vermouth and orange.

ROAST CAULIFLOWER WITH SPICED ALMONDS

SERVES 6–8

700g/1lb 9oz cauliflower
    florets
2½ tbsp olive oil
salt and pepper
1 tsp chopped rosemary
½ tsp chilli flakes
25g/1oz/¼ cup flaked
    (slivered) almonds

Like most brassicas, the cauliflower has been hard done by. Too many of us loathe these princely vegetables, largely, I suspect, as a result of having as children been served them boiled to sulphurous nothing, dished up with nary a pinch of salt or knob of butter. Roasting does them a lot of favours, keeping their texture, avoiding bogginess, and most of all adding a lovely toasty flavour.

UP TO 1 DAY AHEAD (MIN. 30 MINUTES):

Preheat the oven to 220°C/425°F/Gas mark 7. In a roasting pan, toss the cauliflower in 2 tbsp oil and season generously with salt and pepper. Roast for 15–20 minutes, until golden and tender. Leave to cool completely, cover and chill.

Meanwhile, heat the remaining ½ tbsp olive oil in a frying pan over a medium–high heat and add the rosemary, chilli and almonds. Season with a pinch of salt and cook, stirring almost constantly, for about 5 minutes until golden. Tip onto kitchen paper to dry, then store in a bowl.

20 MINUTES AHEAD:

Preheat the oven to 200°C/400°F/Gas mark 6. Warm the cauliflower through for 8–10 minutes (alternatively, stir–fry over a medium heat).

TO SERVE:

Scatter with the almonds and serve.

SCALING UP: Go easy on the chilli flakes.

CURRIED LEEKS WITH LEMON BREADCRUMBS

SERVES 6–8

2 tbsp olive oil

1 garlic clove,
    lightly squashed

100g/3½oz/generous 2 cups
    fresh breadcrumbs

salt and pepper

zest of 2 lemons

a good slice of unsalted
    butter

1 tbsp mild curry powder

1.2kg/2lb 10oz leeks, trimmed,
    halved vertically,
    and sliced about
    5mm/¼in thick

300ml/10fl oz/1¼ cups double
    (heavy) cream

These have been a firm Christmas favourite for years now – they're only very gently curried, but that gives them enough oomph to make the too-often dull leek something of a show-stealer.

UP TO 3 DAYS AHEAD (MIN. 30 MINUTES):

Heat the oil in a frying pan and add the garlic and breadcrumbs. Season with salt and fry until golden, tossing occasionally. Discard the garlic, then stir through the lemon zest. Set aside to cool, then store in an airtight container.

UP TO 1 DAY AHEAD (MIN. 20 MINUTES):

Melt the butter in a good-sized saucepan over a medium heat. Add the curry powder and stir for 30 seconds, then add the leeks and cream. Season with salt and pepper and stir well, then cover and cook over a medium-low heat for 15–20 minutes, stirring occasionally, until soft. Serve hot, or leave to cool, then cover and chill.

15–20 MINUTES AHEAD:

Warm the leeks over a gentle heat with a splash of water, stirring occasionally. Taste for seasoning and add a pinch of salt if necessary.

TO SERVE:

Scatter the lemon breadcrumbs over the leeks and serve.

FREEZABLE

PORT-BRAISED RED CABBAGE

SERVES 6–8

25g/1oz /2 tbsp unsalted
  butter

1 onion, thinly sliced

1 tsp ground ginger

1 tsp ground cinnamon

¼ tsp ground cloves

5 star anise

1 red cabbage, 1kg/2lb 4oz
  or so, quartered, cored,
  and thinly sliced

zest of 1 orange

a little grated nutmeg

300ml/10fl oz/1¼ cups port

100g/3½oz/½ cup soft dark
  brown sugar

100ml/3½fl oz/7 tbsp red
  wine vinegar or
  balsamic vinegar

salt and pepper

I have something of a wintry obsession with red cabbage, and have for years now tried to whittle down a recipe that has that perfect balance of sweet and sour, as well as a deep ruby colour and plenty of spicing. This should tick all those boxes. The addition of port is perhaps somewhat indulgent, but you're not using too much and you certainly don't need an expensive bottle – tawny or LBV will work fine, best even.

This will very much benefit from being made a few days in advance.

UP TO 3 DAYS AHEAD (MIN. 4 HOURS):

Melt the butter in a large saucepan and add the onion. Season with salt and pepper and cook gently for 15 minutes until soft, stirring occasionally. Add the ground spices and star anise and fry over a medium heat for a minute while stirring, then add the remaining ingredients. Give it all a good mix, cover and cook over the lowest heat for 2 hours, stirring now and then. Uncover and cook for a further hour, stirring regularly, until sticky and glossy. Leave to cool, then cover and chill.

30 MINUTES AHEAD:

Reheat the cabbage over a gentle heat, stirring occasionally. Serve.

FREEZABLE

SCALING UP: The spices and port work well as a base to which you can, up to a point, just keep adding cabbage. If it seems too dry, add more port, or a splash of water.

SAUSAGE AND ONION STUFFING

MAKES 20 BALLS

a little olive oil
a big knob of unsalted butter
2 large onions, finely chopped
2 sticks of celery,
    finely chopped
2 garlic cloves, chopped
salt and pepper
a big bunch of parsley,
    finely chopped
7 large sage leaves,
    finely chopped
1 tbsp finely chopped thyme
500g/1lb 2oz sausage meat
150g/5½oz/3 cups fresh
    breadcrumbs

I haven't, you'll have noticed, put the stuffing in with the turkey, both editorially and literally. This is for two reasons. The first is that when it comes to roasting a turkey, it's hard enough to get the timings right without ramming the cavity full of stuffing, and in doing so you're only making your life more difficult. Secondly, it's because if you're doing the *sous vide* turkey on p.96, then there'll be no cavity to stuff, but there's every chance you'll want stuffing nonetheless.

If you want to use this to stuff your turkey then by all means do, but 1) don't fill the cavity entirely and 2) don't pack the stuffing in too tightly – both of these will prevent air circulating around the bird and so skew your cooking times.

UP TO 3 DAYS AHEAD (MIN. 3 HOURS):

Lightly oil a roasting pan.

Melt the butter in a large pan and add the onions, celery and garlic. Season with salt and pepper, cover and cook over a gentle heat for 20 minutes until soft. Cool completely.

Add the herbs, sausage meat and breadcrumbs and stir thoroughly. Form into 20 or so balls, then chill in the fridge for 30 minutes. Meanwhile, preheat the oven to 200°C/400°F/Gas mark 6.

Put the stuffing balls on the oiled roasting pan and bake for 45 minutes. Cool, then cover and chill.

30 MINUTES TO 1 HOUR AHEAD:

Preheat the oven to 200°C/400°F/Gas mark 6. Reheat the stuffing for 15 minutes, then keep warm until ready to serve.

FREEZABLE

CHESTNUT, PINE NUT AND LEMON STUFFING

SERVES 8

50g/1¾oz/4 tbsp unsalted
   butter, plus extra
   for greasing
1 onion, finely chopped
1 garlic clove, finely chopped
1 stick of celery,
   finely chopped
salt and pepper
a pinch of berbere spice
   (optional)
1 tsp chopped thyme
1 tsp chopped rosemary
25g/1oz parsley,
   finely chopped
2 tbsp pine nuts,
   roughly chopped
200g/7oz cooked (vacuum-
   packed are fine) chestnuts,
   finely chopped
125g/4½oz/generous 1 cup
   dried breadcrumbs
zest of 1 lemon
2 eggs, beaten

A vegetarian-friendly, non-sausage-laden stuffing that packs a lovely herbed and fragrant punch. It should please omnivores and vegetarians both.

UP TO 3 DAYS AHEAD (MIN. 2 HOURS):

Melt the butter in a large pan and add the onion, garlic and celery. Season with salt and pepper, cover and cook over a gentle heat for 15–20 minutes until soft. Add the berbere spice, if using, and stir for 30 seconds, then add the thyme, rosemary, parsley, pine nuts, chestnuts, breadcrumbs, lemon zest and eggs, and stir to combine. Taste for seasoning, then leave to cool. Cover and chill.

45 MINUTES AHEAD:

Preheat the oven to 200°C/400°F/Gas mark 6 if necessary (it's most likely already host to another dish or two). Generously grease an ovenproof dish, or 8 muffin tins, with butter. Add the stuffing and bake for 30–40 minutes, until golden on top, then serve.

FREEZABLE

BREAD SAUCE

SERVES 8

1 litre/1¾ pints/4 cups whole
   milk
½ onion, studded with a clove
1 bay leaf
5 peppercorns
150g/5½oz/3 cups fresh white
   breadcrumbs (plus extra
   to thicken, if serving the
   sauce immediately)
50g/1¾oz/4 tbsp butter,
   cubed
salt

This is one of those dishes that really doesn't need mucking around with. No wacky ingredients or alternative techniques are needed, just a little care and a generous hand with the salt and the butter. I'm firmly in the less-is-more camp when it comes to sticking cloves into onions, but if you prefer your onion to resemble a hedgehog then by all means use more.

UP TO 3 DAYS AHEAD (MIN. 30 MINUTES):

Put about three quarters of the milk in a saucepan with the onion, bay leaf and peppercorns, and place over a medium heat. When just below a boil, take off the heat and leave to infuse for 10 minutes, longer if you like – hours even.

Return to a gentle heat and warm through. Remove the onion, bay and peppercorns, and stir in the breadcrumbs and butter. Stir for a few minutes until the butter has melted, then season with salt to taste. It'll be thinner than you probably want but that's fine for now. Leave to cool, then cover and chill. If serving immediately, add a few more breadcrumbs to thicken.

30 MINUTES AHEAD:

Reheat the bread sauce over a low heat. Warm through, stirring gently, and adding a little more milk if necessary.

Warm a serving bowl if by some miracle you have space in the oven.

TO SERVE:

Decant into a warmed bowl and serve.

SCALING UP: 1 bay leaf and 5 peppercorns are ample for greater quantities. Easy on the butter.

CRANBERRY SAUCE

SERVES 12

500g/1lb 2oz/5 cups
    cranberries
200g/7oz/1 cup caster
    (superfine) sugar
zest and juice of 1 lemon
zest and juice of 1 orange
1 cinnamon stick
1 clove

Some versions of this essential sauce verge on the too-sweet, which I'm not convinced is the right way to go. The make-up of the Christmas plate – rich meat, something sausagey, root vegetables and so on – make something sharp and cleansing more appropriate.

UP TO 1 WEEK AHEAD:

Put all the ingredients in a saucepan and bring to a boil, stirring to dissolve the sugar. Simmer gently for 10–15 minutes, until the cranberries have started to burst. Take off the heat and stir briefly. Leave to cool.

Store in sterilized jars (see note on p.200).

FREEZABLE

SCALING UP: No need to add extra spices. Taste as you add the citrus to avoid making it too tart.

HORSERADISH AND ROAST GARLIC CREAM

SERVES 6–8

a bulb of garlic

olive oil

salt and pepper

150ml/5fl oz/⅔ cup double
(heavy) cream

75ml/2½fl oz/5 tbsp buttermilk,
or 40g/1½oz/3 tbsp sour
cream mixed with
3 tbsp milk

25g/1oz fresh horseradish,
grated

2 tsp white wine vinegar

A gussied-up version of horseradish sauce, with the roast garlic adding a lovely sweetness. It's worth getting your hands on fresh horseradish root for this one, though you can buy grated horseradish in a jar from most large supermarkets.

UP TO 3 DAYS AHEAD (MIN. 2 HOURS):

Preheat the oven to 180°C/350°F/Gas mark 4. Cut the top quarter off the garlic bulb, then drizzle the exposed cloves with olive oil and a good pinch of salt. Wrap in foil, then bake in the oven for 45 minutes, until soft and golden. Cool, then squeeze out the cloves into a pestle and mortar or a small blender, and mash until smooth.

Whip the cream to soft peaks, then fold through the garlic, buttermilk, horseradish and vinegar. Season with salt and pepper to taste, cover, and store in the fridge.

GRAVY

MAKES ABOUT 500ML/
18FL OZ/GENEROUS 2 CUPS

For the stock (optional)

a turkey carcass or
    2 chicken carcasses,
    roughly chopped
turkey giblets (optional)
2 onions, halved
a bulb of garlic,
    halved horizontally
1 large carrot,
    roughly chopped
1 leek, roughly chopped
olive oil
salt
1 stick of celery,
    roughly chopped
1 bunch of thyme
1 bay leaf
a few peppercorns

For the gravy

25g/1oz/2 tbsp unsalted
    butter
4 shallots, roughly chopped
salt and pepper
125ml/4fl oz/½ cup dry sherry
    or white wine
1 litre/1¾ pints/4 cups of the
    above stock, or good-
    quality shop-bought stock

A good gravy is one of the crucial building blocks of a successful roast. Made from a decent stock, with a slosh of booze and an intense extraction of roasting juices, it is a great thing; made from gravy granules, not so much. I prefer gravy unthickened, but if you don't, mix a teaspoon of cornflour with a little water and whisk in at the end of cooking.

UP TO 3 DAYS AHEAD (MIN. 6 HOURS):

To make the stock, preheat the oven to 220°C/425°F/Gas mark 7. Put the carcass, giblets, onions, garlic, carrot and leek in a roasting pan. Add a splosh of olive oil and a good pinch of salt and toss thoroughly, then roast for 30–40 minutes until well browned and deliciously roasty.

Transfer this all to a large saucepan along with the celery, thyme, bay leaf and peppercorns, scraping up any juices stuck in the pan. Add water to cover and bring to a boil, skimming off any scum that rises to the surface. Simmer, uncovered, for 2 hours, until reduced by about a half, then leave to cool. Drain through a fine sieve and store in the fridge.

UP TO 1 DAY AHEAD (MIN. 1 HOUR):

Melt the butter in a saucepan and add the shallots. Season with salt and pepper and cook over a low heat until softened. Add the sherry and simmer for 5 minutes, then add the stock and simmer until reduced by half. Pass through a sieve into a clean pan, leave to cool, and store in the fridge. Reheat before serving.

Alternatively, if you're doing this before eating and you have a roast piece of meat ready and resting, put the roasting pan over a medium–high heat and add the sherry. Simmer for a few minutes, scraping up all the caramelized juices, then add all this to the softened shallots along with the stock, and simmer as above, before passing through a sieve. Keep warm until ready to serve.

FREEZABLE

CAKES AND OTHER TREATS

A holiday of plenty such as this wouldn't be complete without a few treats squirrelled away in the cupboard to have with a cup of tea, or for breakfast, or just whenever. As a generally non-sweet-toothed person I nonetheless can't resist the indulgences that come with Christmas. There is, of course, the mince pie, but also panettone and fruit cake and stollen. For those with an aversion to dried fruit, there are German pfefferkuchen (or lebkuchen), Italian ricciarelli, and, perhaps my favourite, some good old American pecan biscuits.

These, like almost all baked numbers, can be made well in advance and kept quite happily in a tin somewhere. Find a Sunday in early December, bung on an apron and the radio, and set to.

PFEFFERKUCHEN

MAKES ABOUT 30

200g/7oz/generous ½ cup
   runny honey
100g/3½oz/7 tbsp unsalted
   butter
zest of 1 lemon
300g/10½oz/scant 2½ cups
   self-raising flour
100g/3½oz/1 cup ground
   almonds
2 tsp ground ginger
1 tsp mixed spice
a good few twists of pepper
a pinch of salt

For the glaze

100g/3½oz/¾ cup icing
   (confectioners') sugar,
   sifted
1 egg white
1–2 tbsp water

Pfefferkuchen, or lebkuchen, are traditional German Christmas cookies. I love their soft texture and festive spicing. They're incredibly easy to make and are a good one with which to get the kids involved.

UP TO 2 WEEKS AHEAD:

Put the honey, butter and lemon zest in a pan over a gentle heat. Mix the dry ingredients in a large bowl. When the butter has melted, beat into the dry ingredients until it forms a stiff dough. Cover and leave to cool completely.

Preheat the oven to 180°C/350°F/Gas mark 4. Line a couple of baking sheets with baking parchment. Taking a little of the dough at a time, roll into a walnut-sized ball, then flatten into a round. Place on the baking sheet and repeat with the remaining dough. Bake for 13–15 minutes, then cool on a wire rack.

For the glaze, whisk together the icing sugar, egg white and water to form a thinnish icing. Using a pastry brush, spread this over the biscuits (or just dip the tops into the icing), then leave to dry. Store in an airtight container.

FREEZABLE

FRUIT CAKE

MAKES 1 LARGE CAKE

250g/9oz/generous 1 cup
  unsalted butter, softened,
  plus extra for greasing
175g/6oz/generous ¾ cup
  dark brown sugar
6 eggs
250g/9oz/2 cups plain
  (all-purpose) flour
1 tsp baking powder
1 tsp fine sea salt
1kg/2lb 4oz/6 cups mixed fruit
  – currants, raisins, sultanas
250g/9oz/2½ cups dried
  cherries
2 tbsp cherry jam
1 tsp ground ginger
1 tsp mixed spice
1 tsp ground cinnamon
1 tsp vanilla extract
1 tsp almond essence
zest of 1 lemon
1½ tbsp glycerine
100ml/3½fl oz/7 tbsp brandy,
  Cointreau, Grand Marnier
  or similar, plus extra for
  subsequent additions
whole blanched almonds,
  to decorate

This recipe comes via mum's friend Janey, and is the best fruit cake I've ever had. Fruit cake haters, of which there are many, have been known to fawn over it. The trick is to bake it in a low oven for several hours, resulting in the juiciest and most moreish fruit cake imaginable.

UP TO 3 MONTHS AHEAD (MIN. 1 WEEK):

Preheat the oven to 140°C/275°F/Gas mark 1. Grease a large springform cake tin and line with greased baking parchment to avoid any risk of sticking.

In a food processor or using an electric whisk (or wooden spoon), cream the butter and sugar until light and fluffy. Beat in the eggs, one at a time, until combined. Fold in the flour, baking powder and salt, and then all the other ingredients, except the almonds, mixing thoroughly. Tip this into the prepared cake tin, then top with the whole almonds and bake for 2½ hours.

Remove from the oven, prick a few times with a skewer, then slosh over a tbsp or two more brandy. Leave to cool completely, then wrap in a couple of layers of baking parchment and store in an airtight container, Every couple of weeks, douse with a couple more tablespoons of booze.

STOLLEN

MAKES 1 LOAF
150ml/5fl oz/⅔ cup whole milk

7g/¼oz (1 sachet) fast-action dried yeast

75g/2¾oz/5 tbsp unsalted butter, softened

75g/2¾oz/⅓ cup caster (superfine) sugar

1 egg

1 tsp fine sea salt

350g/12oz/scant 3 cups strong white bread flour

seeds from 10 cardamom pods, ground

1 tsp mixed spice

100g/3½oz/generous ½ cup dried fruit – raisins and/or sultanas

a handful of glacé (candied) cherries, chopped

150g/5½oz/1 cup chopped mixed peel

150g/5½oz marzipan

To finish

icing (confectioners') sugar

flaked (slivered) almonds

The first stollen was a grim affair. Flour, oats, and water were all that went in it, like some sort of porridge cake. At Christmas, when the Germans wanted to get really fruity, they'd add oil. Yum. It took Pope Innocent VIII to write to the then Prince of Saxony granting him the right to use butter. Alas, the plebs had to pay an annual fee to Rome if they wanted to make their stollen with anything but the ascetic ingredients above, and it wasn't until Saxony became Protestant that butter became more widely used. So Saxony ditched Catholicism in favour of butter, while England did it so that the King could ditch his missus. I think I know whose ends more justified the means.

UP TO 2 WEEKS AHEAD (MIN. 1 DAY):

Warm the milk, add the yeast and leave for a few minutes until frothy. In a large bowl or stand mixer, beat together the butter and sugar until light and fluffy, then beat in the egg. Add the salt, flour and spices, then the yeasty milk. Mix until it comes together, then turn out onto a lightly floured surface. Knead for a few minutes, incorporating all the dried fruit and peel as you knead, until it is light and springy. It'll be fairly sticky to start with but will firm up. Working with slightly wet hands helps. Transfer to a clean bowl, cover, and leave in a warm place for an hour or two, until doubled in size.

Turn out onto a clean, lightly floured surface and gently knock into a flat rectangle. Roll the marzipan into a long sausage shape and lay down the middle of the dough. Fold the dough over the marzipan into a loaf shape, and seal at the edges with your knuckles. Transfer, seam side down, to a lightly floured baking sheet. Cover with a clean tea towel and leave to rise for a further hour, or overnight in the fridge.

Preheat the oven to 180°C/350°F/Gas mark 4. Bake for 35–40 minutes, until golden and firm. Leave to cool for 5 minutes, then transfer to a wire rack to cool. Dust with icing sugar and a scattering of flaked almonds. Serve sliced with a cup of tea, or lightly toasted for breakfast.

FREEZABLE

SCALING UP: Make in 2 separate batches if doubling up.

BOURBON AND MAPLE MINCE PIES

MAKES 12

For the mincemeat

150g/5½oz/scant 1 cup raisins

150g/5½oz/scant 1 cup currants

100ml/3½fl oz/7 tbsp bourbon

200ml/7fl oz/generous ¾ cup maple syrup

zest of 1 lemon

zest and juice of 1 orange

200g/7oz/1½ cups shredded suet

200g/7oz/1¼ cups chopped mixed peel

1 cooking apple, peeled, cored and grated

50g/1¾oz/¼ cup dark brown sugar

2 tsp mixed spice

50g/1¾oz/½ cup flaked (slivered) almonds

a few dashes of orange bitters (optional)

For the pastry

150g/5½oz/generous ½ cup unsalted butter, fridge-cold, cubed

300g/10½oz/scant 2½ cups plain (all-purpose) flour

50g/1¾oz/scant ½ cup icing (confectioners') sugar, plus extra for dusting

zest of 1 lemon

a pinch of salt

75–100ml/2½–3½fl oz/5–7 tbsp cold water

1 egg, beaten

vegetable oil for brushing

Mince pies are generally not something to muck around with. They ought to look like mince pies and taste like mince pies. Which these do, but I've given them the slightest of Yankified tweaks by using bourbon and maple syrup, instead of the more traditional brandy and brown sugar.

This recipe will make far more mincemeat than you need for one batch of mince pies, but it'll keep for an age and, let's face it, you'll need more mince pies, if only for the parfait on p.180.

UP TO 1 MONTH AHEAD (MIN. 1 DAY):

To make the mincemeat, very gently warm the raisins, currants and bourbon in a saucepan for a few minutes, then leave for an hour to plump up. Tip into a bowl and add the remaining ingredients. Mix thoroughly, then cover with a tea towel and leave for a day, stirring whenever you pass. Transfer to a sterilized jar (see note on p.200) and store in a cool, dry place for up to a month, or proceed to mince pie making.

TO MAKE THE MINCE PIES:

To make the pastry, rub the butter into the flour until it resembles breadcrumbs. A food processor is useful here, though not essential. Once combined, add the icing sugar, lemon zest and salt. Add the water a splash at a time and mix until it comes together. Knead briefly to form a dough, but don't overwork. Wrap in clingfilm and chill in the fridge for 30 minutes.

Preheat the oven to 180°C/350°F/Gas mark 4. Lightly brush a 12-hole tartlet tin with vegetable oil.

Roll out the pastry to 3mm/⅛in thick. Using a pastry cutter, cut 12 rounds and sit them in the tartlet tin. Fill with a generous spoonful of mincemeat. Cut 12 smaller rounds, or star shapes (re-rolling the dough if necessary) and sit on top, sealing at the edge. Brush with beaten egg and bake for 25–30 minutes until golden, then transfer to a wire rack to cool. When cool, dust with icing sugar and store in a cool, dry place.

FREEZABLE

CHEAT: Use shop-bought mincemeat. And – why not? – shop-bought pastry.

SCALING UP: You won't need to make more mincemeat.

PANETTONE

MAKES 1 LARGE LOAF

250g/9oz/generous 1 cup
   unsalted butter, softened,
   plus extra for greasing

100g/3½oz/½ cup caster
   (superfine) sugar

zest of 1 large orange

zest of 1 lemon

2 tsp vanilla extract

5 eggs, lightly beaten

14g/½oz (2 sachets) fast-
   action dried yeast

500g/1lb 2oz/4 cups strong
   white bread flour

1 tsp fine sea salt

100ml/3½fl oz/7 tbsp whole
   milk, warmed

100g/3½oz/generous ½ cup
   currants

100g/3½oz/generous ½ cup
   raisins

100g/3½oz/⅔ cup chopped
   mixed peel

1 egg white

icing (confectioners') sugar or
   pearl sugar for dusting

FREEZABLE

SCALING UP: Make in
2 separate batches if
doubling up.

Panettone is one of the most magnificent Christmas treats, and is arguably the most successfully exported festive delicacy, having found its way across the globe certainly more widely than the mince pie. It's best left overnight to prove, being more bread than cake, but is worth the wait. Serve it carved into hunks with custard, toasted for breakfast, or in the bread and butter pudding on p.176.

You probably don't have a panettone tin, but hopefully you'll have a cake tin. Otherwise, you could divide the dough between 8 clean baked bean cans, lined with baking parchment. Bake for 25–30 minutes. Mini panettones make lovely gifts.

UP TO 2 WEEKS AHEAD (MIN. 1 DAY):

Beat the butter and sugar together with the orange zest and lemon zest until pale and fluffy. Beat in the vanilla and then the eggs, a little at a time. If it looks like curdling, add some of the flour, though it's no huge problem if it does split a little.

In a separate bowl, mix the yeast, flour and salt. Make a well in the centre and add the warm milk, whisking in a little of the flour mix, then add the butter and egg mixture. Use a sturdy spoon to bring this all together to form a dough. Make sure it's thoroughly mixed. Cover and chill overnight, or until firm and workable. It will double in size and lose some of its stickiness.

Grease a panettone tin or cake tin with butter, then tie a large piece of baking parchment around the outside.

Lightly flour a work surface and tip the dough out onto it. Add the dried fruit and mixed peel and knead this into the dough, folding and flattening as you go to incorporate all the fruit. Shape into a round and transfer to the prepared cake tin. Cover loosely with clingfilm and leave to rise in a warm place for 2–3 hours, or overnight in the fridge, until trebled in size.

Preheat the oven to 180°C/350°F/Gas mark 4. Brush the top of the panettone with the egg white. Put the tin on a baking sheet and bake for 1¼ hours, covering with foil if it starts to colour too much. The bread is done when a skewer comes out clean.

Remove from the oven. Cool in the tin for 30 minutes, then turn out and cool completely on a wire rack. Dust with icing sugar and store in a cake box or wrapped in baking parchment.

MARMALADE AND GINGER CAKE

SERVES 8

250g/9oz/generous 1 cup
    unsalted butter, softened,
    plus extra for greasing
    (I use the remnants of
    the packet)
250g/9oz/1¼ cups soft dark
    brown sugar
4 large eggs
6 pieces of preserved stem
    ginger in syrup, finely
    chopped, plus 3 pieces,
    chopped, for the top
100g/3½oz/4 tbsp fine-cut
    marmalade, plus 2 tbsp for
    the glaze
2 tbsp black treacle
2 tbsp syrup from the
    ginger jar
250g/9oz/2 cups plain
    (all-purpose) flour
1 tsp baking powder
a pinch of salt

Sticky and festive, but without any dried fruit to speak of (and thus perhaps a relief at this time of year), this is a glorious teatime cake. The recipe is based on one from my wife's book, _The Recipe Wheel_ (Ebury), and is a stonker. I've added preserved ginger, which adds a pleasing texture.

UP TO 1 WEEK AHEAD (MIN. 2 HOURS, IDEALLY 1 DAY):

Preheat the oven to 160°C/325°F/Gas mark 3. Grease a 1 litre/1¾ pint/4 cup loaf tin.

Beat together the butter and sugar until pale and fluffy. One at a time, beat in the eggs, adding a touch of the flour if it looks like curdling (though no problem if it does). Fold in the ginger, marmalade, treacle and ginger syrup, then the flour, baking powder and salt, until combined. Spoon into the loaf tin and bake for 1¼ –1½ hours, until a skewer comes out clean. If it starts to colour too much, cover loosely with foil.

Cool in the tin for 10 minutes, then turn out onto a wire rack. While still warm, glaze the top with the remaining marmalade and sprinkle over the chopped stem ginger.

Serve warm, or leave until cool. Will keep in a cool, dry place for a couple of weeks.

FREEZABLE

DEE DEE'S PECAN DREAMS

MAKES 40 SMALL COOKIES

250g/9oz/generous 1 cup
   unsalted butter, softened
75g/2¾oz/generous ½ cup
   icing (confectioners')
   sugar, plus extra for dusting
250g/9oz/2 cups plain (all-
   purpose) flour
200g/7oz/2 cups pecans,
   finely chopped
1 tsp vanilla extract
1 tsp sea salt flakes
a splash of cold water

Another family Christmas standard – well, there were bound to be plenty, weren't there? – and another that comes from my American grandmother Dee Dee, via mum. These are wonderfully light and nutty biscuits, and dead easy to make. You may need to bake them in two batches.

UP TO 2 WEEKS AHEAD:

Preheat the oven to 180°C/350°F/Gas mark 4. Line a baking sheet with baking parchment.

Usng a wooden spoon or electric whisk, beat together the butter and sugar until pale and fluffy. Stir in the flour, pecans, vanilla and salt, adding a splash of water if necessary to bring together. You should have a stiff dough. Roll the dough into walnut-sized balls, place on the baking sheet and flatten slightly, leaving space in between each. Bake for 12–15 minutes until lightly golden.

Remove from the oven and cool on a wire rack. Dust with icing sugar, and store in an airtight container.

YULE LOG

SERVES 8–10

6 large eggs, separated

150g/5½oz/¾ cup caster (superfine) sugar

50g/1¾oz/7 tbsp unsweetened cocoa powder

a pinch of salt

icing (confectioners') sugar, for dusting

For the filling

100ml/3½fl oz/7 tbsp double (heavy) cream

415g/14oz can unsweetened chestnut purée

2 tbsp brandy

For the icing

150ml/5fl oz/⅔ cup double (heavy) cream

150g/5½oz dark chocolate, broken up

FREEZABLE

SCALING UP: You'll need a larger Swiss roll tin or baking tray, otherwise make the sponge in 2 batches. The filling and icing can be scaled up indefinitely.

Dad's birthday falls just before Christmas, and this has always been his birthday cake. The French are particularly fond of this festive treat, going so far as to make sugar 'mushrooms' to add to the sylvan vibe. By all means adorn this with all the chocolate twigs you like, but you won't find the recipe here. Mine's just a straight-up log, which is to say, a chocolate roulade, gussied up with chestnut filling, chocolate icing and a dusting of snow. Well, icing sugar. It's basically a Swiss roll. Don't tell anyone.

UP TO 3 DAYS AHEAD (MIN. 3 HOURS):

Preheat the oven to 180°C/350°F/Gas mark 4. Grease a 20 x 30cm/ 8 x 12in baking tray or Swiss roll tin and line with baking parchment. Whisk the egg yolks and caster sugar together for a couple of minutes until pale and fluffy. Sift in the cocoa powder and whisk until it comes together. In a spotlessly clean bowl, whisk the egg whites and salt until soft peaks form. Carefully fold this into the chocolate mixture, then just as carefully scrape into the baking tray. Bake for 20–25 minutes until springy to the touch. Leave on the tin to cool for 20 minutes or so. Dust a large piece of baking parchment with icing sugar, and carefully turn the chocolate base onto this. Remove the top layer of parchment.

For the filling, whip the cream until stiff. Fold through the chestnut purée and the brandy. Spread this evenly over the chocolate base. Using the parchment, roll the base lengthways into a long log. Transfer to a large plate or board. If it cracks, panic not. Just pat it together for now. Cut off one end on a diagonal and reposition to form a branch (see photograph). Cover and chill.

For the icing, put the cream in a saucepan over a gentle heat and bring to just short of a boil, then take off the heat. Add the chocolate and leave for a few minutes, then beat with a spoon until smooth and glossy. Leave to cool, then spread all over the chocolate log. Use a fork to make bark-like marks. Cover and chill in the fridge.

TO SERVE:

Dust with icing sugar, cut into fat slices and serve. With more cream if you're feeling particularly decadent.

RICCIARELLI

MAKES 20

200g/7oz/2 cups ground
   almonds
200g/7oz/1¾ cups sifted icing
   (confectioners') sugar, plus
   100g/3½oz/¾ cup
½ tsp baking powder
2 egg whites
1 tsp vanilla extract

These handsome little Sienese almond biscuits are complete heaven. The proper method supposedly involves leaving the unbaked biscuits for 2 days before baking, but I don't quite see the need. They come out beautifully chewy from the egg white, and are a cinch to make.

Serve with vin santo, if you like.

UP TO 2 WEEKS AHEAD:

Preheat the oven to 180°C/350°F/Gas mark 4. Line a baking sheet with baking parchment.

In a large bowl, mix the almonds, 200g icing sugar and the baking powder. In a separate, spotlessly clean bowl, whisk the egg whites until stiff. Add the vanilla extract to the almond mixture, then fold the egg whites through the mixture, using a metal spoon, until combined to form a stiff dough.

Tip the remaining 100g icing sugar onto a baking tray or plate. Taking a small walnut-sized piece of the dough, form into a ball and roll in the icing sugar, then pat it into a flat diamond shape. Shake off any excess sugar and place on the lined baking sheet. Repeat until you have used all the dough. Bake for 12–15 minutes until lightly golden. Remove from the oven and cool on a wire rack. Store in a cool, dry place/airtight container.

FREEZABLE

SCALING UP: These will scale up neatly, though add only ½ tsp vanilla each time you double the recipe.

LEFTOVERS

We hummed and hawed as to whether this chapter needed to be in the book or not. Was this not the antithesis of do-ahead? Do-after, in fact? Well, yes and no. But mostly no – leftovers are for me as much of a Christmas joy as the actual meals themselves, an extraordinary palette of delights with which to paint yet further gastronomic landscapes. Or something.

The turkey sandwich binge has become such a central part of Christmas Day that my siblings and I have started to hold back at lunch in order to leave room for that sainted sanger, with its stuffing and cranberry sauce and layer of gravy-soaked bread in the middle (this, as any *Friends* fan will know, is called 'the moist maker').

But there's more to leftovers than sandwiches, and I hope within this chapter you'll find some inspiration for turning the Christmas–New Year lull into some fine eating.

TURKEY PHO

For the broth

2 onions, halved and peeled

a few fat slices of fresh ginger

5 star anise

2 cinnamon sticks

1 tsp fennel seeds

2 cloves

1 Thai chilli, chopped

turkey or chicken bones, or a
chicken stock cube

3 tbsp fish sauce

1 tbsp caster (superfine) or
palm sugar

For the soup

300g/10½oz vermicelli rice
noodles

300g/10½oz or so leftover
turkey, shredded

a big handful of coriander
(cilantro) leaves

a big handful of Thai basil, or
mint leaves

50g/1¾oz beansprouts

6 lime wedges

4 Thai chillies, chopped

Sriracha hot sauce (optional)

Pho **is a Vietnamese noodle soup, thus making it pretty much the perfect tonic to jaded, hungover Christmas palates. It's fresh and lively and deeply nourishing.**

UP TO 3 DAYS AHEAD (MIN. 3 HOURS):

Make the broth: put a large, heavy-bottomed pan over the highest possible heat. Add the onion and the ginger. Burn them. Really burn them. Add the star anise, cinnamon, fennel, cloves, chilli, turkey bones, fish sauce and sugar. Cover with water and bring to a boil. Simmer for 2–3 hours, until reduced by half. Strain and leave to cool, then chill, or continue to the next step.

Cook the noodles according to packet instructions, then cool in a bowl of iced water before draining.

30 MINUTES AHEAD:

Put the broth over a medium heat. When hot, add the turkey to warm through. Taste the broth and add salt if necessary.

Warm some large bowls.

TO SERVE:

Divide the noodles between the bowls. Spoon over the broth. Garnish with the herbs, beansprouts, lime and chillies, and serve.

SCALING UP: Thai chillies are punchy, so go easy with them. For more broth just add extra water, a stock cube and a little more fish sauce to taste.

TURKEY FRICASSEE

SERVES 6–8

25g/1oz/2 tbsp butter
2 onions, finely sliced
2 garlic cloves, sliced
2 sticks of celery,
 finely chopped
2 leeks, halved vertically
 and sliced
salt and pepper
2 tbsp mild curry powder
2 tbsp plain (all-purpose)flour
150ml/5fl oz/⅔ cup dry sherry
750ml/1¼ pints/3 cups
 chicken or turkey stock
3 tbsp raisins
1–1.5kg/2½–3½lb leftover
 turkey, shredded
150ml/5fl oz/⅔ cup double
 (heavy) cream

To serve
boiled rice
mango chutney
coriander (cilantro) leaves
flaked (slivered) almonds

This is one of the dishes without which Christmas really wouldn't be Christmas. Mum's version is a variation of Claire Macdonald's recipe, and is, for some reason, usually served with tagliatelle. My wife Rosie deemed the combo 'a bit weird' at her first family Christmas, so perhaps you'd be better off with rice. Or a baked potato. Either way, it's an irresistible dish.

UP TO 2 DAYS AHEAD (MIN. 1 HOUR):

Melt the butter in a large pan. Add the onions, garlic, celery and leeks. Season with salt and pepper, cover, and cook over a low heat for about 30 minutes, stirring occasionally, until completely softened.

Turn up the heat a touch, and add the curry powder. Stir for a minute or so, then add the flour, and stir for another minute. Now add the sherry and simmer for a couple of minutes, stirring to thicken. Add the stock and bring up to a gentle boil, then add the raisins and the leftover turkey. Simmer for 30 minutes, then stir in the cream and cook for another minute or two. If not serving immediately, leave to cool, cover and chill.

30 MINUTES AHEAD (IF NECESSARY):

Gently reheat the fricassee.

TO SERVE:

Serve with rice and mango chutney and garnish with coriander and flaked almonds,

FREEZABLE
SCALING UP: If making a larger batch, you won't need to go too wild with the vegetable base, nor the cream.

TURKEY AND HAM PIE

SERVES 6–8
25g/1oz/2 tbsp butter
1 onion, sliced
2 fat leeks, split down the
    middle and finely sliced
salt and pepper
2 tbsp plain (all-purpose) flour
700ml/1¼ pints/scant 3 cups
    chicken, turkey or
    ham stock
600–800g/1lb 5oz–1lb 12oz
    cooked turkey, cubed
600–800g/1lb 5oz–1lb 12oz
    cooked ham, cubed
a big bunch of parsley,
    finely chopped
2 tbsp chopped tarragon
375g/13oz puff pastry
1 egg, beaten

Those days between Boxing Day and New Year's Eve can sometimes feel like dead air space, a sort of festive limbo. I say fill that limbo with pie.

UP TO 2 DAYS AHEAD (MIN. 2 HOURS):
Preheat the oven to 190°C/375°F/Gas mark 5.

Melt the butter in a large pan and add the onion and leeks. Season with salt and pepper and sweat for 20 minutes until soft. Stir in the flour and cook for a couple of minutes, then add the stock, a little at a time at first while stirring. Simmer for a minute or two until it thickens, then add the meat. Simmer for 5 minutes, stir in the herbs, and taste for seasoning. Take off the heat.

Grease a pie dish and fill with the turkey and ham. Roll out the pastry on a lightly floured surface to about 3mm/⅛ in thick. Cover the pie dish with the pastry, trim around the edges, then brush with egg and score a few times with the blunt side of a knife. Poke a little hole in the top to let some air out, and bake for 40 minutes. Serve, or leave to cool, then chill.

TO REHEAT:
Bake for 25–30 minutes at 200°C/400°F/Gas mark 6.

FREEZABLE

TURKEY FATTEE

SERVES 6

300–500g/10oz–1lb 2oz
   cooked turkey, shredded

For the chilli sauce

2 tbsp unsalted butter

1 tsp ground coriander

1 tsp ground cumin

½ tsp ground cinnamon

½ tsp sweet smoked paprika

1 tsp chilli flakes

500ml/18fl oz/2 cups passata
   (strained tomatoes)

2 tbsp red wine vinegar

1 tsp sugar

salt and pepper

For the garlic yogurt

300g/10½oz/1¼ cups thick
   plain yogurt

1 garlic clove, crushed to
   a paste

olive oil

For the pitta crisps

50g/1¾oz/4 tbsp butter

3 pitta breads

For the rice

250g/9oz/ generous 1¼ cups
   basmati rice

2 tbsp olive oil

400g/14oz canned
   chickpeas, drained

1 cinnamon stick

3 star anise

500ml/18fl oz/generous 2 cups
   chicken stock

To finish

a big handful of fresh mint,
   coriander (cilantro)
   and parsley

Fattee is a Lebanese dish of layered crisp pitta bread, rice, chilli sauce, garlic, yogurt, herbs … need I go on?

UP TO 3 DAYS AHEAD (MIN. 1 HOUR):

Make the chilli sauce: melt the butter over a medium heat and add the spices and chilli flakes. Stir for a minute, then add the passata, vinegar and sugar. Season and simmer for 20 minutes, stirring occasionally, until thickened. Set aside.

Beat the crushed garlic into the yogurt with a good pinch of salt and a slug of olive oil. Store in the fridge.

UP TO 1 DAY AHEAD:

For the pitta crisps, preheat the oven to 200°C/400°F/Gas mark 6. Melt the butter. Lightly toast the pittas in a toaster, then halve them through the middle so you have six thin pieces. Brush with butter and bake in the oven for 8 minutes, until golden. Sprinkle with sea salt then store somewhere handy.

1 HOUR AHEAD:

Preheat the oven to 180°C/350°F/Gas mark 4. Toss the turkey with olive oil, salt and pepper. Put in a baking dish, cover with foil, and bake for 20 minutes until hot. Keep warm.

30 MINUTES AHEAD:

Gently reheat the chilli sauce.

Rinse the rice under running water for a few minutes, then shake dry, or dry-ish. Heat the oil in a large pan and add the rice. Stir for a couple of minutes over a good heat until lightly toasted, then add the chickpeas, spices, and chicken stock. Bring to a boil, cover, and simmer very gently for 12 minutes without removing the lid. Take off the heat and leave for another 5 minutes, still covered. Now uncover and leave for a couple of minutes before fluffing up with a fork.

TO SERVE:

Layer up, starting with a pitta crisp, then the rice, then the turkey, followed by chilli sauce and garlic yogurt. Garnish with a big handful of fresh herbs and serve.

PILAF

600–800g/1lb 5oz–1lb 12oz
  leftover turkey, shredded
200 g/7 oz/generous ¾ cup
  Greek-style yogurt
1 garlic clove, crushed to
  a paste
2 green chillies, deseeded
  and finely chopped
1 tbsp grated fresh ginger
1 tsp ground coriander
500g/1lb 2oz/2½ cups
  basmati rice
2 tbsp vegetable oil
1 cinnamon stick
1 tsp black mustard seeds
1 dried red chilli
10 curry leaves (optional)
1 onion, finely chopped
1 garlic clove, finely sliced
salt and pepper
1 tsp ground turmeric
1 litre/1¾ pint/4 cups chicken
  stock
To servet
fresh coriander (cilantro)
plain yogurt
mango chutney

This is a lovely, aromatic way to use up leftover meat. It will work with pretty much anything you have, though turkey is particularly good.

UP TO 1 DAY AHEAD:

Put the turkey in a bowl with the yogurt, garlic, green chillies, ginger and ground coriander and leave to marinate for as long as you can.

45 MINUTES AHEAD:

Rinse the rice in a sieve under running water for a couple of minutes, until the water runs clear. Drain in a sieve.

Heat the oil in a large pan and add the cinnamon, mustard seeds, dried chilli and curry leaves and stir for a minute or so until the seeds start to pop, then add the onion and garlic, season with salt and pepper, and cook, stirring regularly, until soft and golden.

Add the turmeric, the turkey and its marinade to the pan and keep stirring until it starts to colour, then add the rice. Stir to coat it in the spicy mixture, then add the stock and bring to a boil. Cover and cook over a low heat for 12 minutes without removing the lid.

Take off the heat, leaving the lid on, and rest for 5 minutes. Remove the lid and leave to steam for a minute or two before fluffing up with a fork. Serve with fresh coriander, yogurt and mango chutney.

STOCK

MAKES 2 LITRES
turkey or chicken bones
3 onions, halved and peeled
a bulb of garlic,
    halved horizontally
2 carrots, sliced thickly
2 tomatoes, halved
2 tbsp grapeseed or
    groundnut (peanut) oil
salt and pepper
a few sprigs of thyme
1 bay leaf
4 litres/7 pints/4 quarts water

A delicious, deeply flavoured and rich stock is one the most useful things you can have in the fridge. It takes seconds to make (at least, in terms of hands-on time) and will be a great ally for soups, gravies and stews. I generally like my stocks really roasted and browned, though if you like something lighter, you can omit the roasting of the bones.

Preheat the oven to 200°C/400°F/Gas mark 6. Put the bones, onions, garlic, carrots and tomatoes in a large roasting pan. Toss in the oil and a good pinch of salt and pepper. Roast for 1 hour, shaking every 20 minutes, until roasted and golden.

Transfer to a large saucepan and add the thyme and bay leaf. Cover with the water, then bring to a boil, skimming off any scum that rises to the surface. Simmer gently for 2–3 hours, until reduced by half. Strain through a sieve, leave to cool, then cover and chill. It'll keep for 3 days.

FREEZABLE

SALAD OF GOOSE OR DUCK WITH ORANGE AND WATERCRESS

**SERVES 6–8 AS A STARTER OR
4 AS A LIGHT MAIN**

1 orange
100g/3½oz watercress
about 20g/¾oz parsley leaves
leftover roast goose or duck,
    shredded or sliced
a few chopped hazelnuts,
    toasted
a handful of pomegranate
    seeds

For the dressing

2 tsp Dijon mustard
a tiny garlic clove, crushed to
    a paste
a sprig of thyme
2 tbsp red wine vinegar
6 tbsp olive oil
salt and pepper

The simplest of salads, but a rather luxurious one nonetheless.

UP TO 1 DAY AHEAD:

Make the dressing by shaking all the ingredients together in a jar;
set aside.

UP TO 6 HOURS AHEAD:

Using a small, sharp knife, slice off the orange peel, taking off
all the white pith but taking care not to whip off too much flesh.
Slice the orange into thin rounds, then tear into small pieces.
Cover and chill.

TO SERVE:

Toss the watercress and parsley leaves together with the
dressing. Garnish with the duck or goose, orange, hazelnuts and
pomegranates, and serve.

ROOT VEGETABLE AND CHEESEBOARD COBBLER

SERVES 6–8

splash of olive oil

1 onion, finely chopped

1 garlic clove, finely chopped

25g/1oz/2 tbsp butter

25g/1oz/3 tbsp plain (all-purpose) flour

500ml/18fl oz/generous 2 cups whole milk, warmed

150–200g/5–7oz cheese, crumbled, rinds discarded

800g–1kg/1lb 12oz–2lb 4oz cooked root vegetables, cut into chunks

For the cobbler topping

150g/5½oz/generous ½ cup very cold unsalted butter

300g/10½oz/scant 2½ cups self-raising flour

2 tbsp chopped herbs – parsley, rosemary, thyme, whatever you have

salt and pepper

100ml/3½fl oz/7 tbsp cold water

1 egg, beaten

At the risk of implying a recipe of mine amounts to some kind of gastronomic landfill, this – like the rumbledethumps opposite – is quite a nifty means of using up the odds and ends from Christmas lunch. Trim the rinds off your leftover cheese bits and bung 'em in. It is in no way a refined dish, but it's a delicious and hearty one.

UP TO 3 DAYS AHEAD (MIN. 90 MINUTES):

Preheat the oven to 180°C/350°F/Gas mark 4.

Heat the oil in a large pan and cook the onion for about 10 minutes, until soft. Add the garlic and stir for a minute, then add the butter. When the butter has melted, add the plain flour and stir for another minute until combined, then pour in the milk a splash at a time until thickened. Stir in the cheese to melt, then add the vegetables. Taste for seasoning and adjust if necessary before taking off the heat. Transfer to a lightly buttered ovenproof dish.

For the cobbler topping, coarsely grate the butter into the flour, then rub together to combine. Stir in the herbs along with a pinch of salt, then the cold water. Briefly knead to bring together, then roll out on a lightly floured surface to about 1cm/½in thick. Cut into rounds, then knead and repeat with the off-cuts. Top the vegetables with the cobbler discs. Brush with beaten egg, then bake for 40–50 minutes until golden. Serve, or leave to cool, then cover and chill.

TO REHEAT:

Warm in an oven at 180°C/350°F/Gas mark 4 for 30 minutes.

FREEZABLE

RUMBLEDETHUMPS

MAKES 6
1 tbsp olive oil
1 onion, chopped
salt and pepper
1 garlic clove, chopped
250g/9oz cooked cabbage
    or Brussels sprouts,
    finely shredded
400–500g/14oz–1lb 2oz
    cooked root vegetables,
    such as potatoes,
    parsnips, carrots

Rumbledethumps are the Scottish equivalent of bubble and squeak: leftover potatoes mashed with cooked cabbage and onion, and baked until golden. At Christmas this can essentially become a graveyard – though a handsome graveyard – for a lot of leftover vegetables. Roast potatoes, carrots, parsnips, sprouts, whatever you have lying around – it can go in, and it'll be delicious. Eat for breakfast with some sausages or for supper with, well, anything.

AT SOME POINT AHEAD, IF NECESSARY:
Fry the onion in the oil with salt and pepper, until soft and golden. Add the garlic and shredded cabbage and cook for another couple of minutes, stirring regularly. Mash together the vegetables and add the onions and cabbage. Season with salt and pepper and combine thoroughly. Form into patties and store in the fridge or freezer until needed.

1 HOUR AHEAD:
Preheat the oven to 200°C/400°F/Gas mark 6. Grease an ovenproof dish with a little butter or oil and pop in the patties. Bake for 30–40 minutes, until crisp and golden. Serve.

FREEZABLE

PANETTONE BREAD AND BUTTER PUDDING

SERVES 6–8

400ml/14fl oz/scant 1¾ cups double (heavy) cream

400ml/14fl oz/scant 1¾ cups whole milk

1 vanilla pod, split down the middle

4 egg yolks

150g/5½oz/¾ cup caster (superfine) sugar

600g/1lb 5oz panettone, fatly sliced and buttered

a little softened butter, for greasing

demerara sugar

This recipe is entirely adaptable, in that you can really use any old bread for it, but panettone should add a nip of luxury, as well as plenty of flavour. Where with a classic B & B P you tend to add orange zest and currants and the like, with a panettone they're already incorporated into the bread.

Adapt quantities to fit amount of panettone you have (one vanilla pod will be ample, mind), though honestly you don't need to be too precise here.

UP TO 3 DAYS AHEAD (MIN. 1 HOUR):

Preheat the oven to 160°C/325°F/Gas mark 3. Lightly grease a large baking dish and sit it in a large roasting pan.

Put the cream, milk and vanilla in a pan and bring to a boil over a medium heat. Meanwhile, in a large, heavy bowl, whisk together the egg yolks and caster sugar until pale and fluffy. When the cream and milk are just below a boil, add them to the egg yolks, whisking all the time. Remove the vanilla.

Put a layer of buttered panettone in the baking dish, then pour over some of the custard. Continue until you've used it all up. Pour boiling water into the roasting pan to come halfway up the side of the baking dish. Bake for 45 minutes, until a crust has formed but the centre still has a little wobble. Serve, or leave to cool, cover and chill.

TO REHEAT (IF NECESSARY):

Reheat at 180°C/350°F/Gas mark 4 for 20 minutes.

FREEZABLE

GOOSE-FAT FRIED CHRISTMAS CAKE WITH STILTON

FOR 1 SERVING

2 tsp goose fat

a slice of Christmas cake, marzipan discarded if necessary

a hunk of Stilton

chopped walnuts (optional)

You'll want to discard the marzipan and icing, if there is any, before embarking on this healthy treat. It works nicely with the Christmas pudding, too.

Melt the goose fat over a medium–high heat. Add the Christmas cake and fry for a couple of minutes on each side, until crisp and hot. Serve with Stilton and a few chopped walnuts if you like.

MINCE PIE PARFAIT

SERVES 8–10

600ml/20fl oz/2½ cups double
   (heavy) cream
juice of 1 lemon
2 egg whites
100g/3½oz/½ cup caster
   (superfine) sugar
250g/9oz mince pies,
   thoroughly chopped up
100g/3½oz/¾ cup toasted
   hazelnuts or almonds,
   chopped
zest of 1 orange
100ml/3½fl oz/7 tbsp brandy
   (optional)

I would quite happily make a batch of mince pies specifically for the purpose of making this dessert. Or, at least, make more than I need in order to have some leftover.

UP TO 3 DAYS AHEAD (MIN. 6 HOURS):

Whip the cream and lemon juice until stiff. In a separate bowl, whisk the egg whites until stiff peaks form, then slowly whisk in the sugar until you have a thick, glossy meringue. Fold this into the whipped cream, then fold in the mince pies, toasted nuts, orange zest and brandy.

Line a 1 litre/1¾ pint/4 cup loaf tin or cake tin with clingfilm, then spoon in the parfait mix. Wrap tightly and freeze for a minimum of 6 hours.

TO SERVE:

Turn the parfait out onto a board, cut into slices, and serve.

CHRISTMAS PUDDING ICE CREAM

SERVES 6–8

600ml/20fl oz/2½ cups double
   (heavy) cream
100g/3½oz/½ cup caster
   (superfine) sugar
1 vanilla pod
4 egg yolks
200–300g/7–10oz leftover
   Christmas pudding,
   finely crumbled
zest of 1 lemon

Leftover Christmas pudding has a habit of sitting around for some days before finding its way to the bin. This is a good way of breaking that habit. Best eaten within a couple of days.

UP TO 3 DAYS AHEAD (MIN. 6 HOURS):

Put the cream, sugar and vanilla in a pan and slowly bring to a boil, stirring to dissolve the sugar. Whisk the egg yolks in a large, heavy bowl. When the cream is at a rolling boil, tip onto the yolks, whisking furiously. Once incorporated, leave to cool.

Pick out the vanilla pod and fold through the Christmas pudding and lemon zest, then churn in an ice-cream machine, or put in the freezer. Whip up with a fork after 4 hours and return to the freezer until ready to serve.

EDIBLE PRESENTS

Presents are lovely. Presents you can eat are even better. At the risk of descending into cliché and platitude, giving a loved one something you've gone to the effort of making, as opposed to just buying in a rush on Christmas Eve, shows a great deal of care and thought. A jar of pickled pears will trump a voucher most days of the week; a box of Champagne truffles will deliver you straight to page one of Aunt Myrtle's good books; and a bottle of damson gin will go one better than that. And I don't know about you, but I'd rather spend an hour in the kitchen making something delicious, than an hour traipsing around in the rain, jostling with other shoppers, and standing in a queue.

PICCALILLI

MAKES 4 X 370G/13OZ JARS

400g/14oz small cauliflower
    florets
200g/7oz runner beans,
    cut on a diagonal
200g/7oz green beans,
    cut on a diagonal
200g/7oz shallots,
    roughly chopped
200g/7oz red onion,
    finely sliced
100g/3½oz fine sea salt
2 tbsp mustard oil or
    groundnut (peanut) oil
2 tbsp yellow mustard seeds
1 garlic clove,
    very finely chopped
2 tsp ground ginger
1 tbsp ground turmeric
2 tbsp English mustard
    powder
4 tbsp plain (all-purpose) flour
500ml/18fl oz/generous 2 cups
    cider vinegar
100g/3½oz/½ cup caster
    (superfine) sugar

This British stab at an Indian pickle from way-back-when has seen something of a renaissance of late. For some time it sat in the gastronomic doldrums, but in tandem with the re-emergence of the Scotch egg, piccalilli is now back on the pub menu, and I'm glad it is. Its union of crunch, spice, tang and sweetness is just what you need with the Christmas cold cuts.

UP TO 6 MONTHS AHEAD (MIN. 1 DAY):

Put all the vegetables in a large bowl and add the salt. Fill with water, swish around to dissolve, then leave for an hour or two. Drain thoroughly.

Heat the oil in your biggest pan and add the mustard seeds. Stir for a few seconds until they start to pop, then add the garlic and spices. Stir for a further 30 seconds, then stir in the flour and a splash of vinegar until it forms a paste. Slowly add the remaining vinegar, whisking to ensure there are no lumps, then add the sugar, continuing to whisk until smooth and lightly simmering. Add the vegetables and stir well, then simmer for 10–15 minutes, stirring occasionally, until just softening. Take off the heat and leave to cool, then spoon into sterilized jars (see note on p.200) and store in a cool, dry place.

It will keep for up to 6 months.

SCALING: If making a smaller batch this will halve neatly. Likewise for a larger batch, though you won't need more mustard oil.

NOUGAT

rice paper
85g/3oz/scant ¾ cup runny
    honey
250g/9oz/1¼ cups granulated
    sugar
3 tbsp water
2 large egg whites
200g/7oz/generous 1½ cups
    shelled pistachios
100g/3½oz/⅔ cup chopped
    mixed peel

These make pretty little presents, and could also be served after dinner. The trick is to keep whisking and keep whisking some more. An electric whisk will be invaluable. If you can't find rice paper (online and in large supermarkets), leave to set on baking parchment lightly rubbed with a little vegetable oil, and chill in the fridge.

UP TO 2 WEEKS AHEAD (MIN. 1 DAY):

Line a small baking tray with rice paper.

Put the honey, sugar and water in a pan over a low heat, stirring until the sugar has dissolved. Increase the heat and simmer rapidly until it reaches 160°C/325°F – this should take 5–7 minutes. A sugar thermometer is helpful, but if you don't have one, drop a little of the mixture into cold water – it is ready when it separates into brittle threads (the 'hard crack' stage). Remove from the heat.

In a clean, dry bowl, whisk the egg whites until stiff, preferably using an electric whisk. Pour in the hot light caramel, whisking continually. Keep whisking for several minutes until you can whisk no more – it should be very thick indeed. Fold through the nuts and mixed peel, then tip into the baking tray and smooth flat. Top with another layer of rice paper and cool completely. Cut into slices and store in a cool, dry place/airtight container.

CHESTNUT JAM

MAKES 2 X 300G/10FL OZ JARS

400g/14oz cooked, peeled
    chestnuts
200g/7oz/1 cup caster
    (superfine) sugar
1 tsp vanilla extract
3 tbsp honey
3 tbsp bourbon or brandy
1 tsp sea salt flakes

This is an utterly delicious and versatile Christmas treat. If you have a surfeit of fresh chestnuts then you'll need to spend some time peeling them – cut a cross in the top, boil for 3 minutes, drain, cool and peel – but in this recipe you can use vacuum-packed chestnuts. Much easier. Use as a doughnut filling, in cakes, or in the filling for the yule log (p.157).

UP TO 3 MONTHS AHEAD (MIN. 1 DAY):

Put the chestnuts in a saucepan, add water to cover and simmer gently for 20 minutes until tender. Drain, reserving the cooking water, and blend in a food processor with a good splash of that water, until smooth.

Put another good splash of the cooking water in the saucepan along with the sugar, and stir over a medium heat until dissolved. Add the chestnut purée, vanilla, honey, bourbon and sea salt, and stir to combine. Simmer very gently for 5 minutes (it tends to spit), stirring regularly. Take off the heat and leave to cool for a few minutes. Decant into sterilized jars (see note on p.200) and store in a cool, dry place.

CHAMPAGNE TRUFFLES

MAKES 30–40

300ml/10fl oz/1¼ cups double (heavy) cream

200g/7oz dark chocolate, broken into small pieces

100g/3½oz milk chocolate, broken into pieces

50g/1¾oz/4 tbsp unsalted butter, softened

3 tbsp Champagne

To finish

100g/3½oz dark chocolate, broken into small pieces

100g/3½oz/generous ¾ cup shelled pistachios, finely ground

Homemade truffles are among the easiest and most impressive things to make. I've added a touch of festive luxury here with the Champagne addition, but you really don't need to crack open a bottle if you don't want to – a splash of brandy works, or even just a pinch of sea salt. As fine a gift as there can be. Or, you know, just eat them yourself.

UP TO 2 WEEKS AHEAD (MIN. 8 HOURS):

Put the cream in a small pan over a medium–low heat and slowly bring to a boil. When on the point of simmering, take it off the heat and add the chocolate and butter. Leave to melt for 2 minutes, then stir until smooth and glossy. Add the Champagne and stir thoroughly. Cover and chill in the fridge for 6 hours.

Using a pair of teaspoons and your hands, gently form the truffle mixture into balls. Return to the fridge for 30 minutes, or the freezer for 10 minutes.

To finish, melt the chocolate in a bowl over a pan of gently simmering water. Meanwhile, put the ground pistachios on a plate and line a baking sheet with a piece of baking parchment. Dip the truffles in the melted chocolate, then lightly roll in the pistachios. Transfer to the baking sheet and leave in the fridge until set. Store in a cool, dry place.

FREEZABLE

SCALING UP: Add ½ part Champagne each time you double.

PICKLED PEARS

**MAKES 1 LARGE (1 LITRE/
1¾ PINT/4 CUP) JAR**

300g/10½oz/1½ cups caster
    (superfine) sugar
500ml/18fl oz/generous 2 cups
    white wine vinegar
1 tsp salt
1 cinnamon stick
2 star anise
2 cloves
1 tsp fennel seeds,
    lightly crushed
1 bay leaf
6 pears

**These are particularly sensational with blue cheese, though go
very well indeed with ham, pork pies and the like, or just tossed
through a salad.**

UP TO 6 MONTHS AHEAD (MIN. 1 DAY):

Put the sugar and vinegar in a large pan and gently bring to a
boil, stirring to dissolve the sugar. Add the salt, spices and bay leaf
and simmer for 5 minutes. Peel the pears and add to the pan,
then simmer for 45 minutes. Take off the heat and leave to cool.

Transfer the pears to a sterilized jar (see note on p.200) along
with the pickling juice, and close the lid securely. Store in a cool,
dry place.

SCALING UP: This quantity of spices should make themselves
known even in greater quantities.

DAMSON GIN

MAKES A BOTTLE
about 300–400g/10–14oz
   damsons
300g/10½oz/1½ cups caster
   (superfine) sugar
70cl bottle of good-quality
   gin, or vodka

If you're a fantastically organized Christmas present shopper and you're reading this in October, then you've come to the right place. If it's Christmas Eve then you'd be better off with one of the other recipes in this chapter. This needs time. Not much of yours, but time for the damsons to infuse the gin, and of course you'll need to pick the damsons in the autumn.

This isn't a means of masking crap gin. Use crap gin and you'll have crap damson gin.

2 MONTHS AHEAD:

Put the damsons in a freezer bag and freeze for a day. Bash enthusiastically with a rolling pin, then transfer to a sterilized 1.5 litre/2½ pint/6 cup jar (see note on p.200). Add the sugar and the gin and shake thoroughly to dissolve the sugar. Store in a cool, dry place for a minimum of two months. Give the jar a shake every day or so for the first couple of weeks, then whenever you remember for the subsequent weeks. It'll be happy for years.

When ready, strain into a clean bottle.

GREEN TEA SHORTBREAD

MAKES 30 BISCUITS

200g/7oz/generous ¾ cup
    unsalted butter, softened
100g/3½oz/¾ cup icing
    (confectioners') sugar
2 egg yolks
200g/7oz/generous 1½ cups
    plain (all-purpose) flour
100g/3½oz/1 cup ground
    almonds
4 tsp matcha green tea
    powder, or green
    tea leaves
1 tsp sea salt flakes
2–3 tbsp golden caster
    (superfine) sugar

If you can get hold of matcha green tea – easily ordered online – then these are beautifully and vividly green. Otherwise, green tea leaves will give a lovely flavour, if not colour. You'll need to grind them in a pestle and mortar until fine, ideally.

UP TO 1 WEEK AHEAD (MIN. 4 HOURS):

Cream the butter and icing sugar together until pale, then add the egg yolks and beat until smooth. Stir in the flour, almonds, tea and salt, and briefly knead to bring together, but don't overwork. Transfer to a clean surface and form into an even sausage shape with a 5–7cm/about 2½in diameter. Wrap in clingfilm and chill for 30 minutes.

Preheat the oven to 180°C/350°F/Gas mark 4. Line a baking sheet with baking parchment. Scatter the caster sugar in a separate baking tray and roll the dough in it to coat. Slice into 1cm/½in thick biscuits and place on the baking sheet. Bake for 13–15 minutes until lightly golden. They may feel soft but they'll firm up as they cool. Leave to cool on the baking sheet for 5 minutes, then transfer to a wire rack to cool completely.

When cool, transfer to an airtight container.

CHOCOLATE-COVERED ORANGE PEEL

MAKES ABOUT 40 PIECES

2 large oranges

200g/7oz/1 cup caster
(superfine) sugar

200ml/7fl oz/generous ¾ cup
water

100g/3½oz dark chocolate,
broken into pieces

50g/1¾oz/7 tbsp pistachios,
finely ground

This recipe was inspired by my friend Ravinder Bhogal, a brilliant cook, terrific writer and lovely person.

UP TO 2 WEEKS AHEAD (MIN. 6 HOURS):

Using a sharp knife, score the orange peel in quarters, then peel off. Cut each piece into 5 strips. Boil these for 10 minutes. Drain and boil again for another 5 minutes. Drain. This takes the bitter edge off the orange.

Put the sugar and water in the pan and bring to a boil, stirring to dissolve the sugar. Add the orange peel and simmer very gently for 45 minutes–1 hour, swirling the pan every now and then, until the liquid is very thick and sticky and coating the peel. Remove with a pair of tongs or chopsticks and leave to dry on a wire rack or baking parchment for a few hours, or overnight.

When the peel is dry, melt the chocolate in a heatproof bowl over a pan of barely simmering water. Put the pistachios in a bowl. Dip the orange pieces in the chocolate to coat half of each, then roll the chocolatey bit in the ground pistachios. Dry on a sheet of baking parchment, then store in a cool dry place.

INDEX

ACKNOWLEDGEMENTS

Thank you to Polly Powell, Emily Preece-Morrison, and everyone at Pavilion Books, for their continued support, encouragement, enthusiasm and insight. A giant panettone of thanks to Clare Winfield for the beautiful photography, to Rosie Reynolds for styling the food so well, and an extra mince pie to prop stylist extraordinaire Wei Tang to celebrate the third book we've done together. A particularly large glass of tangerine whiskey sour to Maggie Ramsay for, yet again, her sharp eye and gentle suggestions, and another mince pie for the hat-trick. A huge slice of fruitcake for Jennifer Christie and Jane Graham Maw. An extra-large wedge of stollen to my supper club partner Sam Herlihy, who knows how to gild a lily without ruining it. Love and thanks to my in-laws, Rod and Sue, for letting me take over their kitchen last Christmas in the name of recipe testing. And last but by no means least, to my wife Rosie, the angel atop my Christmas tree.

First published in the United Kingdom in 2014 by
Pavilion Books Company Ltd
1 Gower Street, London W14 0RA

Copyright © 2014 Pavilion Books
Text copyright © 2014 James Ramsden
Photography copyright © 2014 Pavilion Books

ISBN: 978-1-90981-542-1

A CIP catalogue record for this book is available from the British Library

10 9 8 7 6 5 4 3 2 1

Reproduction by Dot Gradations, United Kingdom
Printed and bound by 1010 Printing International Ltd, China

Commissioning editor: Emily Preece-Morrison
Designer: Laura Russell and Emma Wicks
Photographer: Clare Winfield
Food stylist: Rosie Reynolds
Stylist: Wei Tang
Copy editor: Maggie Ramsay

NOTES

1 teaspoon = 5ml; 1 tablespoon = 15ml.
All spoon measurements are level.

Medium eggs are used, except where otherwise specified. Free-range eggs are recommended. Note that some recipes contain raw or lightly cooked eggs. The young, elderly, pregnant women and anyone with an immune-deficiency disease should avoid these, because of the slight risk of salmonella.

To sterilize jars for pickles, sauces and jams, first scrub the jars clean, then place in a preheated oven at 110°C/225°F/Gas mark ¼ for 1 hour.